# THE DUCHESS OF BLOOMSBURY STREET

ALSO BY HELENE HANFF
84, Charing Cross Road
Apple of My Eye
Letter from New York
Q's Legacy
Underfoot in Show Business

# THE DUCHESS OF BLOOMSBURY STREET

## Helene Hanff

3 1489 00455 2491

MOYER  BELL

Wakefield, Rhode Island & London

Published by Moyer Bell
Fourth Printing, 1998

Copyright © 1973 by Helene Hanff

All rights reserved. No part of this publication may be reproduced or transmitted in any form or by any means, electronic or mechanical, including photocopying, recording, or any information retrieval system, without permission in writing from Moyer Bell, Kymbolde Way, Wakefield, Rhode Island 02879 or 112 Sydney Road, Muswell Hill, London N10 2RN.

---

**LIBRARY OF CONGRESS
CATALOGING-IN-PUBLICATION DATA**

Hanff, Helene, 1916-1997. The Duchess of Bloomsbury Street
p.    cm.

1. Hanff, Helene—Journeys—England.   2. Women authors, America—20th century—Biography.   3. Booksellers and bookselling—England.   4. England—Description and travel.
5. Americans—Travel—England.   I. Title.

PS3515.A4853Z464                1995
818'.5409—dc20                  95-505
                                CIP
ISBN 1-55921-144-X

---

Printed in the United States of America. Distributed in North America by Publishers Group West, 1700 Fourth Street, Berkeley CA 94710, 800-788-3123 (in California 510-528-1444)

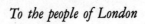

*To the people of London*

# THE DUCHESS OF BLOOMSBURY STREET

Theoretically, it was one of the happiest days of my life. The date was Thursday, June 17, 1971; the BOAC lifted from Kennedy airport promptly at 10 A.M.; the sky was blue and sunny, and after a lifetime of waiting I was finally on my way to London.

But I was also fresh out of the hospital after unexpected surgery, I was terrified of going abroad by myself (I am terrified of going to Queens or Brooklyn by myself; I'm afraid of getting lost) and I had no idea what I would do if something went wrong and nobody met the plane. I especially didn't know how I would manage the mammoth borrowed suitcase I couldn't budge, let alone carry.

Year after year I'd planned a pilgrimage to London, only to have it canceled at the last minute by some crisis, usually financial. This time it was different. From the beginning, heaven seemed to favor the trip.

I'd written a book called *84, Charing Cross Road*, and a few months after it came out in New York, a London publisher named André Deutsch bought it for publication in England. He wrote me that the London edition would be brought out in June and he wanted me there to help publicize the book. Since he owed me a small "advance," I wrote and told him to keep the money in his office for me. I figured it was enough to keep me in London for three weeks if I was frugal.

In March, the *Reader's Digest* bought an article I wrote about my fan mail and the *Digest* check bought the BOAC ticket, some expensive clothes and—as things turned out—an expensive surgeon.

With the surgery, contributions came in from all over. The Democratic Club I belong to didn't send flowers to the hospital, they sent a Harrods gift certificate. A friend just back from London stuck a wad of British pounds under my door labeled "For theatre tickets." And one of my brothers stopped by and gave me a hundred dollars "to go to Paris with." I had no intention of going to Paris (I never wanted to see any city but London) but the hundred meant an extra week in London plus a few frills like cabs and hairdressers. So financially I was all set.

The night before I left, two friends gave me a farewell party. I'd spent the day packing, to the indignant fury of all my vital organs, and I left the party early and was in bed and asleep by midnight. At 3 A.M. I came staring awake, with my insides slamming around and a voice in my head demanding:

"What are you *doing*, going three thousand miles from home by yourself, you're not even HEALTHY!"

I got out of bed, had hysterics, a martini and two cigarettes, got back in bed, and whiled away the rest of the night composing cables saying I wasn't coming.

Paul, the doorman, drove me to the airport. I got on the passport line holding my coat, scarf, magazines and an extra sweater in one hand, while the other held up the pants of my new navy pantsuit which had refused to stay up by themselves since the operation.

Standing in line proved to be no more uncomfortable than hanging by my thumbs, and when I was finally allowed to board the plane I slid into my seat by the window blissful in the knowledge that for five hours I wouldn't have to move a muscle. Somebody brought me sandwiches and coffee I hadn't had to make; somebody brought me a martini; and somebody else was going to clean it all up afterwards. I began to relax.

When I was completely relaxed, the voice in my head inquired what I planned to do if something went wrong and nobody met the plane. To forestall panic, I got the letters out of my shoulder bag and read them over. Those letters were my lifeline.

The first was from Carmen, André Deutsch's publicity girl.

Dear Helene,

I've confirmed your reservation for June 17th at the Kenilworth Hotel. It's just up the way from Deutsch's so you won't feel too alone. The publication date of your book is June 10th, sorry you'll miss it but glad you're on the mend.

We're all looking forward to seeing you on the 18th.

Thanks to a mix-up I had two hotel rooms, one at the Kenilworth and one at the Cumberland. On the advice of well-traveled friends I'd hung onto both rooms in case one wasn't there for me when I arrived. But I was going to the Kenilworth first; it was cheaper.

The second letter was a hasty, last-minute scrawl from Nora Doel. *84, Charing Cross Road* is the story of my twenty-year correspondence with Marks & Co., a London bookshop, and particularly with its chief buyer, Frank Doel, whose sudden death had given rise to the book. Nora is his widow; Sheila is his daughter.

Helene—

Sheila and I will be at Heathrow Airport on Thursday night at ten. We're both very excited.
Have a good trip.

Nora

The third letter came from an Englishman who had written me a fan letter after he read *84, Charing Cross Road* and had asked when I was finally coming to London. I wrote and told him, and he wrote back:

I am a retired publisher now working at London Airport. Please, if I can be of help, USE ME! I can meet you off your plane and see you through Customs and Immigration. Any friends meeting you would have to meet you AFTER you leave Customs. I would meet you off the plane before your dainty feet touched British soil.

I hadn't the slightest idea how he expected to manage it but I was counting heavily on his getting my dainty feet off the plane. What did I know about Customs and Immigration?

There was a fan letter from the wife of an American professor working at Oxford for a year, inviting me to visit them at Oxford. There was a fan letter from an American living in London, who wanted to take me on a walking tour. And there was a letter from Jean Ely, a retired actress in New York whom I'd met as a result of the book:

Dear Helene:

I've written to a friend in London about you. He's an Old Etonian who knows London better than anyone I ever met. I've never imposed on him in this way before but I wrote him you were one visitor he must take on a tour of London. His name is Pat Buckley. He'll get in touch with you at the Kenilworth.

I won't tell you to have a wonderful time, you couldn't possibly have anything else.

Jean

P.S. Keep a diary. So much will be happening to you, you won't remember it all without a diary.

I read all the letters over several times. I checked my passport and vaccination certificate several times; I studied an English Coins card somebody had given me, and I read a BOAC booklet I hadn't had time to read before, on What to Take With You on the Trip. It listed twenty-three items, fourteen of which I didn't have:

3 washable dresses
2 vests
2 pair gloves

small hat(s)
twin set
wool stole
evening dress
evening bag
evening shoes
girdle.

I'd brought three pantsuits, two skirts, several sweaters and blouses, a white blazer and one dress. The dress was silk, chic and expensive, it had a matching coat and was intended to cover large evenings.

I got out my Visitors' Map of London and pored over it. I can read maps only in terms of Up, Down, Left and Right, but I'd marked key places—St. Paul's, Westminster Abbey, the Tower of London—and I'd charted walking tours all over the map. The key places would have to wait till the end of my stay, when I hoped to be able to stand still for long periods, but meanwhile I could walk the city end to end. (I'd discovered I was all right as long as I kept moving.)

I was perfectly calm and happy until a voice announced over the intercom that it was 9:50 P.M. British time, we would be landing at Heathrow Airport in five minutes and it was raining in London.

"Don't panic," I told myself. "Just decide *now* what you'll do if Nora and Sheila aren't there and that nut at the airport forgot this is the day you're coming."

I decided I would look up Nora and Sheila Doel in the phone book and call them. If they didn't answer I would look up Carmen of Deutsch's. If she didn't answer I would go up to an airport official and say:

"Excuse me, sir. I have just arrived from New York, I have a suitcase I can't budge, I don't know where the Kenilworth Hotel is and I am Not Well."

The plane began its descent and the passengers moved about, collecting hand luggage. I had no hand luggage. I sat frozen and told myself that if nobody met me I would sit in the airport till the next plane left for New York and fly home. At which moment the voice spoke again into the intercom:

"Will Miss Hanff please identity herself to a member of the staff?"

I leaped to my feet and held up my free hand (one hand being permanently attached to the pants) only to find there wasn't a member of the staff in sight. The other passengers, lining up to leave the plane, stared at me curiously as, red-faced but awash with relief, I gathered up everything in my free hand and got on the end of the line. Now that I knew I was being met, I was giddy and half drunk with excitement. I had never really expected to make it to London—and I'd made it.

I reached the stewardess who was saying goodbye to disembarking passengers, and told her I was Miss Hanff. She pointed to the bottom of the ramp and said:

"The gentleman is waiting for you."

And there he was, a big, towering Colonel Blimp with a beaming smile on his face and both arms outstretched, waiting to get my dainty feet onto British soil. As I went down the ramp to meet him, I thought:

"Jean was right. Keep a diary."

*Thursday, June 17*
*Midnight*

There's a radio in the headboard of this bed, the BBC just bid me goodnight. The entire radio system here goes to bed at midnight.

Arrival triumphant.

"Helene, my dear!" boomed the Colonel, stooping to kiss me on the cheek, nobody would have believed he'd never set eyes on me before. He's a beaming giant of a man with tufted gray eyebrows and tufted white sideburns, and a vast stomach that marches on ahead of him; and he strode off to see to my suitcase ramrod straight, a Sahib out of Kipling's Old Injah. He came back, followed by a porter with the suitcase on a trolley, put an arm around me and walked me past the Immigration and Customs tables, calling genially to the men behind them, "Friend of mine!" and that was all I saw of Immigration and Customs.

"Now then," he said. "Are you being met?"

I told him Nora and Sheila Doel were there somewhere.

"What do they look like?" he asked, scanning the crowd jammed behind a rope that cordoned off the arrival area.

"I have no idea," I said.

"Have they a snapshot of you?" he asked.

"No," I said.

"Do they know what you're wearing?" he asked.

"No," I said.

"But my dear girl!" he boomed. "How did you expect to find them?! Wait here."

He parked me in front of an Information Desk and strode off. A moment later, a voice over the public-address system asked Mrs. Doel to come to the Information Desk—and a pretty, black-haired woman ducked under the cordon directly in front of me, thrust a sheaf of roses in my arms and kissed me.

"Sheila said it was you!" said Nora in a rich Irish brogue. "We saw every woman off the plane. I said, 'That one's too blond,' and, 'That one's too common.' Sheila just kept sayin', 'It's the little one in the blue trouser suit, she looks so excited.'"

The Colonel steamed up and got introduced, and we went out to Nora's car. She and Sheila got in front, I got in back and the Colonel announced he would follow in his car, unless Sheila would rather he led? Did she know the way to the Cumberland?

"The Kenilworth," I corrected. I explained about the two hotel rooms and the Colonel stared at me in horror.

"Well, in that case," he bellowed, "some total stranger at the Cumberland has a roomful of beautiful roses!"

He drove off to the Cumberland to reclaim his roses and I drove off toward the Kenilworth with Nora's roses in my arms, thinking, "It was roses, roses, all the way," and trying to remember who wrote it.

It was dark and rainy as we drove along a highway that might have been any highway leading to any city, instead of the road to the one city I'd waited a lifetime to see. Nora was lecturing me for not staying with her and Sheila in North London ("Frank always meant you to stay with us!"), and as we entered London both of them pointed out the sights:

"There's Piccadilly!"

"This is the West End."

"This is Regent Street." And finally, from Sheila:

"You're on Charing Cross Road, Helene!"

I peered out at the darkness, wanting to say something appropriate, but all I could see were narrow wet streets and a few lighted dress-shop windows, it could have been downtown Cleveland.

"I'm here," I said. "I'm in London. I made it." But it wasn't real.

We drove on to Bloomsbury and found the Kenilworth on the corner of a dark street. It's an old brownstone with a shabby-genteel lobby, it's going to suit me.

I registered and the young desk clerk handed me some mail, and then Nora and Sheila and I rode up to inspect Room 352. It looked pleasant and cheerful with the drapes drawn against the rain. Nora surveyed it judiciously from the doorway and announced:

"It's gawjus, Helen."

"My name's Helene," I said.

She looked surprised but unimpressed.

"I've been calling you 'Helen' for twenty years," she said, peering into the bathroom. It has a shower stall but no tub. "Look at this Sheila, she's got her own loo!"

The loo is the toilet, Sheila thinks it comes from Waterloo.

We went back down and found the Colonel fuming in the sleepy lobby: he'd found his roses lying half dead on the Cumberland Package Room floor and had had a row with the management.

We went into the dining room, empty but still open, and the Colonel located a young Spanish waiter who said his name was Alvaro and allowed we could have sandwiches and tea-or-coffee.

"You smoke too much, Helen," Nora announced, after we ordered.

"I know it," I said.

"You're too thin," she went on. "I dunno what kind of bloke that surgeon is, to let you come away so soon after your op. A hysterectomy is a very serious op."

"Is it, Mum," said Sheila mildly in her university accent. She and Nora exchanged a look, and Nora giggled. They're remarkable, they talk in code and finish each other's sentences, you'd never guess they were stepmother and daughter. Sheila's an attractive girl in her twenties, laconic and unruffled. ("Just like Frank," Nora told me.)

Nora was much struck by the fact that she and the Colonel were both widowed two years ago. He has one child, a daughter who's being married in the country on Saturday.

"Now, why don't you three girls put on your prettiest dresses and come to the wedding?" he invited expansively. "It's going to be a superb wedding!"

I declined and Nora obviously didn't think she should go if I didn't, so she declined, too, wistfully. ("I don't know him, Helen," she said when I got her alone. And I said: "Who knows him?!")

They left at eleven. Nora said she would give me tomorrow to rest and would call me Saturday about the interview. ("We're being interviewed together by the BBC! You've made us all famous!")

The Colonel said he'd be in the country for a week and would call me when he got back and "arrange a little trip into our glorious countryside."

I came up and unpacked a few things and climbed into bed with the mail.

Postcard from Eddie and Isabel, old friends from back home. They'll be in town Monday and will pick me up to go sight-seeing.

A note from Carmen at Deutsch's:

Welcome!

I know you're going to be very tired but I'm afraid we have a journalist from the Evening Standard along to see you here at 10 A.M. tomorrow. Someone will be by to pick you up before 10.

On Saturday at 2:30, the BBC want to interview you and Mrs. Doel on "The World This Weekend."

On Monday at 3:30 an interview on "The Woman's Hour," also at Broadcasting House.

On Tuesday, visits to bookshops, including Marks & Co. (closed but still standing, and we want photos of you there), and at 2:30 an Autograph Party next door at 86 Charing Cross Road, Poole's Bookshop.

On Tuesday evening, André Deutsch will give a dinner for you to meet the Deutsch officers and a distinguished journalist.

I just got uneasy about remembering all those dates, and got out of bed and made a day-to-day calendar out of a pocket memo book. I'm also uneasy about how I'm going to break the news to Carmen that I don't have my picture taken. I'm neurotic, I don't like my face.

I lie here listening to the rain, and nothing is real. I'm

in a pleasant hotel room that could be anywhere. After all the years of waiting, no sense at all of being in London. Just a feeling of letdown, and my insides offering the opinion that the entire trip was unnecessary.

*Friday, June 18*

The alarm clock went off at eight and I got out of bed and went to the window to see if it was still raining. I pulled back the drapes—and as long as I live I'll never forget the moment. From across the street a neat row of narrow brick houses with white front steps sat looking up at me. They're perfectly standard eighteen- or nineteenth-century houses, but looking at them I knew I was in London. I got lightheaded. I was wild to get out on that street. I grabbed my clothes and tore into the bathroom and fought a losing battle with the damnedest shower you ever saw.

The shower stall is a four-foot cubicle and it has only one spigot, nonadjustable, trained on the back corner. You turn the spigot on and the water's cold. You keep turning, and by the time the water's hot enough for a shower you've got the spigot turned to full blast. Then you climb in, crouch in the back corner and drown. Dropped the soap once and there went fifteen dollars' worth of hairdresser down the drain, my shower cap was lifted clear off my head by the torrent. Turned the spigot off and stepped thankfully out—into four feet of water. It took me fifteen minutes to mop the floor using a bathmat and two bath towels, sop-it-up, wring-it-out, sop-wring, sop-wring. Glad I shut the bathroom door or the suitcase would have been washed away.

After breakfast, I went out in the rain to look at those houses. The hotel is on the corner of Great Russell and Bloomsbury Streets. It fronts on Great Russell, which is a commercial street; the houses I saw from my window are on Bloomsbury.

---

I walked slowly along the street, staring across it at the houses. I came to the corner, to a dark little park called Bedford Square. On three sides of it, more rows of neat, narrow brick houses, these much more beautiful and beautifully cared for. I sat on a park bench and stared at the houses. I was shaking. And I'd never in my life been so happy.

All my life I've wanted to see London. I used to go to English movies just to look at streets with houses like those. Staring at the screen in a dark theatre, I wanted to walk down those streets so badly it gnawed at me like hunger. Sometimes, at home in the evening, reading a casual description of London by Hazlitt or Leigh Hunt, I'd put the book down suddenly, engulfed by a wave of longing that was like homesickness. I wanted to see London the way old people want to see home before they die. I used to tell myself this was natural in a writer and booklover born to the language of Shakespeare. But sitting on a bench in Bedford Square it wasn't Shakespeare I was thinking of; it was Mary Bailey.

I come of very mixed ancestry, which includes an English Quaker family named Bailey. A daughter of that family, Mary Bailey, born in Philadelphia in 1807, was the only ancestor I had any interest in when I was a little girl. She left a sampler behind and I used to stare at that sampler, willing it to tell me what she was like. I don't know why I wanted to know.

Sitting in Bedford Square I reminded myself that Mary Bailey was born in Philadelphia, died in Virginia and never saw London. But the name persisted in my head. Maybe she was a namesake. Maybe it was her grandmother or great-grandmother who had wanted to go home again. All I knew, sitting there, was that some long-dead Mary Bailey or other had finally found a descendent to go home for her.

I came back here and fixed myself up so I'd make a good impression on Deutsch's. Brushed my navy suit jacket (which they will flatly refuse to believe back home) and spent half an hour tying my new red-white-and-blue scarf in an ascot so I'd look British. Then I went down to the lobby and sat bolt upright in a chair by the door, afraid to move for fear of mussing myself, till a young secretary blew in to escort me three doors up Great Russell Street to Deutsch's.

I met Carmen—very brisk and efficient and dramatic-looking—and got interviewed by a bouncy young reporter from the *Evening Standard* named Valerie Jenkins. After the interview the three of us and a photographer piled into a cab, and Carmen said to the driver:

"Eighty-four Charing Cross Road."

I felt uneasy, knowing I was on my way to that address. I'd bought books from 84 Charing Cross Road for twenty years. I'd made friends there whom I never met. Most of the books I bought from Marks & Co. were probably available in New York. For years, friends had advised me to "try O'Malley's," "try Dauber & Pine." I'd never done it. I'd wanted a link with London and I'd managed it.

Charing Cross Road is a narrow, honky-tonk street, choked with traffic, lined with second-hand bookshops. The open stalls in front were piled with old books and maga-zines, here and there a peaceful soul was browsing in the misty rain.

We got out at 84. Deutsch's had stuffed the empty window with copies of the book. Beyond the window the shop interior looked black and empty. Carmen went next door to Poole's and got the key and let us in to what had once been Marks & Co.

The two large rooms had been stripped bare. Even the heavy oak shelves had been ripped off the walls and were lying on the floor, dusty and abandoned. I went upstairs to another floor of empty, haunted rooms. The window letters which had spelled Marks & Co. had been ripped off the window, a few of them were lying on the window sill, their white paint chipped and peeling.

I started back downstairs, my mind on the man, now dead, with whom I'd corresponded for so many years. Halfway down I put my hand on the oak railing and said to him silently:

"How about this, Frankie? I finally made it."

We went outside—and I stood there and let them take my picture as meekly as if I did it all the time. That's how anxious I am to make a good impression and not give anybody any trouble.

When I came back to the hotel there was a letter at the desk. From Pat Buckley, the Old Etonian Jean Ely wrote to about me.

No salutation, just:

Jean Ely writes that you are here on your first visit. Can you have a bite of supper here on Sunday at 7:30?— and we will drive around and see a bit of old London.

Call me Saturday or Sunday before 9:30 A.M.

In haste—
P.B.

*Saturday, June 19*

Totally demoralized.

Just came up from breakfast and phoned Pat Buckley.

"Oh, yes," he said in a very U accent, "Hallo."

I told him I'd love to come to supper tomorrow night and asked if there were other people coming.

"I'm not giving a supper party for you!" he said impatiently. "Jean wrote me you wanted to see London!"

I stammered that I was glad we'd be alone, I'd only asked so I'd know how to dress; if we were alone I could wear a pantsuit.

"Oh, Lord, must you?" he said. "I loathe women in trousers. I suppose it's old-fashioned of me but I do think you all look appalling in them. Oh well, I suppose if you must, you must."

It's fifty degrees here and raining, I'm not climbing into a summer skirt for him.

Nora just phoned, she'll pick me up at two this afternoon for the interview.

"You're right behind the British Museum, Helen," she said. "Go sit in the Reading Room, it's very restful."

Told her I see enough museums in New York, and God knows I sit in enough Reading Rooms.

Will now slog out in the wet and tour Bloomsbury.

*Midnight*

Nora and I were interviewed at Broadcasting House, it's the only big modern building I've seen here and I hope I don't see another one; it's a monstrosity—a huge semicircular block of granite, it looks obese. They don't understand skyscrapers here. In New York they don't understand anything else.

The interviewer was choice. First she told the radio audience that though Nora and I had corresponded over a twenty-year period we'd never met. Then she turned to us and asked us what we thought of each other: now that we'd met, were we disappointed? If we'd never corresponded and had just met, would we like each other?

"Now what kind of question was that to ask me?" Nora demanded when we came out. "How-would-I-like-you-if-we'd-just-been-introduced. How do I know whether I'd have liked you or not? I've known you for twenty years, Helen!"

She drove me out Portland Place and through the Regent's Park section, which I loved passionately on sight. We passed Wimpole Street and Harley Street—and there I was in a *car*, I felt as if I were locked in a metal container and couldn't get out, but it was raining. I'm going back there on foot the first dry day.

There's a Crescent of Nash houses—I'm not too clear about when Nash lived but he built tall white opulent houses reeking of Beau Brummell and Lady Teazle—and when the rain stopped for a little we got out of the car and sat on a park bench so I could stare at the Crescent. We chose which houses we'll buy if we're born rich next time.

Nora told me she came to London as a poor servant girl from Ireland before the war. She worked in one of the houses of the gentry as a kitchen maid, cutting paper-thin bread for the cucumber sandwiches.

She drove me home to Highgate for dinner. She and Sheila bought a house out there after Frank died and the younger daughter married. We drove past Hampstead Heath on the way, and Nora stopped the car at the cemetery where Karl Marx is buried. The gates were locked but I peered over the wall at him.

Their house is high in the hills of North London on an attractive suburban street that blazes with roses, every house has a rose garden in full bloom. The roses here are as wildly colored as a New England autumn: not just red, pink and yellow, but lavender roses, blue roses, purple and orange roses. Every color has a separate fragrance, I went berserk smelling my way around Nora's garden.

We had strawberries and thick English cream for dessert, and when Nora came to her last berry she looked up at Sheila, stricken, and said:

"It came out 'never' again, Sheila!"

She eats berries to the old children's rhyme to find out when she's going to marry again: "This year, next year, sometime, never." When it comes out "never," Sheila has to comfort her. Sheila's much more like Nora's mother than her stepdaughter.

Nora cut a fresh armload of roses for me, and Sheila drove me home. She teaches in a suburban school. There are two men who take her out; I think both of them bore her, she still hasn't met one she wants to marry.

Big excitement in the lobby when I came in because of the *Evening Standard* interview; one of the desk clerks had saved a copy for me.

Excerpt:

She steps into London, frightfully trim in a chic navy trouser-suit from Saks and a foulard tied French-style.

Kill yourself tying an ascot and it comes out French-style. Story of my life.

You can't imagine how funny it strikes me when somebody calls me chic. I'm wearing the same kind of clothes I've worn all my life and for years I was looked on as a bohemian mess. My sister-in-law Alice, for instance, used to wear herself out every year trying to find a shoulder bag to give me for Christmas because I wouldn't carry a handbag and nobody else wore shoulder bags so no manufacturers made them. (Handbags make you choose between your wallet, your glasses and your cigarettes. Choose two of the three and maybe you can get the bag closed.) I also wouldn't wear high heels because I like to walk, and you can't walk if your feet hurt. And I lived in jeans and slacks because skirts are drafty in winter and hamper you when you walk, and besides, if you're wearing pants nobody knows there's a run in one stocking.

So for years I was this sartorial horror who ran around in low heels, pants and shoulder bags. I still run around that way—and after a lifetime of being totally out of it, I'm so With it my pantsuit gets a rave review in the *Evening Standard*.

*Sunday, June 20*

Sallied forth with my map after breakfast and saw the sights of Bloomsbury. Got lost several times; it seems a street can be on the Left on your map without necessarily being Left of where you're standing. Various gents came out from under umbrellas to point me where I wanted to go.

It cleared after lunch and I'm now in a neighborhood park, lying in a deck chair soaking up the fog. There are three handkerchief-sized parks very close to the hotel. This one's just beyond the British Museum. Sign on the gate says:

---

### RUSSELL SQUARE

———

PLEASE DON'T LEAVE LITTER

———

PERSONS WITH DOGS
ARE REQUIRED TO KEEP THEM
UNDER PROPER CONTROL.

———

---

There's a rose garden in the middle of the square encircling a very practical birdbath: a marble slab with a thin jet of water in the center. A bird can stand around and drink or wash his feathers without drowning. Wish whoever designed it would go to work on the English shower problem.

An elderly gentleman in uniform just came up, bowed and said:

———

"Fourpence, please."

For the use of the deck chair.

He was apologetic about the weather, he and I are the only ones out here. I said the rain was good for the roses, and he told me the gardeners in London's squares compete every year for the honor of growing the best roses.

"I do think this year our chap has a chance," he said. Told him I would definitely root for the Russell Square gardener.

Have to go put on the navy suit for Pat Buckley. Or I may just be mean and stay in my second-best coffee-brown on account of the weather.

*Midnight*

I've been sitting on the edge of the bed for an hour in a complete daze. I told him if I die tonight I'll die happy, it's all here, everything's here.

Pat Buckley lives in Rutland Gate, it's down in Knightsbridge or Kensington below the left-hand edge of my Visitors' Map, I took a cab. Rutland Gate is a small compound of white stone houses round a green square. Everything in London is round a green square, they're like small oases everywhere.

He has a ground-floor flat. I rang the bell and he opened the door and said:

"Hallo, you found it all right."

He's slight—thin build, thin face, indeterminate age—and he has one of those light, almost brittle, English voices, pleasant but neutral. He took my jacket and ushered me into an Oscar Wilde drawing room. There's a full-length portrait of his mother in her court-presentation gown on one wall. On another wall, a glass cabinet houses his collection of gentleman's calling-card cases—small square cases, gold, silver, onyx inlaid with pearl, ivory worked with gold filligree, no two alike. The collection is his hobby and it's dazzling.

He brought me sherry, and when I told him I found Eton very glamorous he brought me his Eton class book and showed me photos of his rooms there.

We had supper in the dining room at a polished mahogany table set with heavy English silver. He has a "daily" who leaves a cold supper for him and his guests and makes the coffee and sets the table before she leaves. The place setting was the same as at home—fork at the left, knife and spoon at the right—but lying horizontally above the dinner plate were an oyster fork and a soup spoon. I let him go first so I could see what you did with them.

We had chicken salad followed by strawberries and cream—and that's what you use them for: you spear a strawberry with the oyster fork, scoop cream up on the soup spoon, transfer the berry to the spoon and slurp.

After supper we climbed into his car. He didn't ask what I wanted to see, he just drove me to the corner where the Globe Theatre stood. Nothing is there now, the lot is empty. I made him stop the car and I got out and stood on that empty lot and I thought the top of my head would come off.

He got out of the car then, and we prowled the dark alleys nearby—Shakespeare's alleys, still there. And Dickens' alleys: he pointed to an Artful Dodger peering furtively out the window of an ancient pile of stone.

He took me to a pub called The George, and as he opened the door for me he said in that light, neutral voice:

"Shakespeare used to come here."

I mean I went through a door Shakespeare once went through, and into a pub he knew. We sat at a table against the back wall and I leaned my head back, against a wall Shakespeare's head once touched, and it was indescribable.

The pub was crowded. People were standing at the bar and all the tables were full. I was suddenly irritated at all those obtuse citizens eating and drinking without any apparent sense of where they were, and I said snappishly:

"I could imagine Shakespeare walking in now, if it weren't for the people."

And the minute I said it I knew I was wrong. He said it before I could:

"Oh no. The people are just the same."

And of course they were. Look again, and there was a blond, bearded Justice Shallow talking to the bartender. Further along the bar, Bottom the Weaver was telling his ponderous troubles to a sharp-faced Bardolph. And at a table right next to us, in a flowered dress and pot-bellied white hat, Mistress Quickly was laughing fit to kill.

He dragged me out of there and drove me to see St. Paul's by floodlight. I wanted at least to walk up the steps and touch the doors of John Donne's cathedral but it will be there tomorrow, there's time, there's time.

He drove me to the Tower of London, more huge and terrifying than I'd imagined, like a sprawling medieval Alcatraz. We got there just at ten, so I could watch the guards lock the Tower gates. For all their flashy black-and-scarlet uniforms, they are grim and frightening as they lock the gates to that dread prison with darkness closing in. You think of the young Elizabeth sitting somewhere behind the stone walls wanting to write and ask Bloody Mary to have her beheaded with a sword instead of an ax.

When the gates were locked, the guards marched back toward the huge iron Tower door. It rose to let them pass through, lowered and clanged shut behind them, and the light voice beside me said:

"They haven't missed a night in seven hundred years."

The mind boggles. Even going back only three hundred years, you think of London during the Great Fire, the Great Plague, the Cromwell revolution, the Napoleonic wars, the First World War, the Second World War—

"They locked the Tower with all this ceremony," I asked him, "every night, even during the Blitz?"

"Oh yes," he said.

Put THAT on Hitler's tombstone, tell THAT to that great American patriot, Wernher von Braun, whose buzz bombs destroyed every fourth house in London.

When he drove me home and I tried to thank him, he said:

"Oh, thank *you!* Most Americans won't take this tour. They'll drive around with me for a quarter of a hour and then they want to know where the Dorchester Bar is."

He said most Americans he knows never see London.

"They take a taxi from the Hilton to Harrods, from Harrods to the theatre, from the theatre to the Dorchester Bar."

He said he knows four American businessmen who've

been in London for a week without ever leaving the Hilton.

"They stay shut up in their rooms all day with the telephone and a bottle of Scotch, you wonder why they ever left the States."

He gave me a list of sights to see but didn't suggest showing them to me himself.

*Monday, June 21*

Eddie and Isabel picked me up this morning to go sight-seeing. Isabel is an old school friend, they live in Texas. They are the most conventional, conservative people I know.

It was sunny this morning, and when they came for me the sight of them charmed me: Isabel wore cotton overalls and a print blouse, Eddie was in a sports shirt and slacks. It was the first time I'd ever seen them that they didn't look ultra proper-and-respectable. I had an interview at Broadcasting House at three and I thought I might not get back here first so I wore my marked-down beige linen pantsuit; next to them I was overdressed.

They'd been to London before and had seen the sights so we just wandered around the shopping district all morning. They like to window-shop and buy curios and good prints and we did that. At lunch time, we were wandering along a street when I stopped suddenly and gawked because there, directly ahead of us, was Claridge's.

Claridge's is where all the characters in Noel Coward lunch. For years I've had glamorous images of fashionable London sailing grandly into Claridge's—and there before my eyes was today's fashionable London still sailing grandly into Claridge's.

Eddie asked what I was staring at and I explained.

"Fine," he said promptly. "We'll have lunch at Claridge's."

It was a spontaneous, generous gesture very typical of him. I waited for Isabel to say, "Now Eddie, not the way we're dressed!" but to my astonishment, she didn't.

"I think it's very fancy," I said. "Let's go home and change first."

"They'll take our money," said Eddie dryly—and took our arms and led us proudly into Claridge's.

I'm a slob by nature. On an ordinary day at home I couldn't care less how I look. But this was CLARIDGE'S. I sat through lunch in that room of grace and elegance surrounded by tables of perfectly groomed Londoners— sandwiched between two happy Texans dressed for a picnic and affectionately pleased at having taken me somewhere special.

After lunch they went with me to Broadcasting House, and then more window shopping, and at six we were in the theater district. A few people were on line at the Aldwych hoping for last-minute return tickets to *A Midsummer Night's Dream*. Eddie spoke to a man on line and came back and said:

"There are always a few returns. If we get on line now, we can get tickets at seven, when the box office opens. It's a seven-thirty curtain, we'll eat afterwards."

This was the Peter Brook production, you understand, the National Shakespeare Theater Company production. I would have given a week of my life for a ticket. I'd tried to get them for Nora and Sheila and me through the hotel, it was the one show I couldn't get, it's sold out for the rest of the run. And much as I wanted to see it, I *couldn't* have walked into that theater looking the way we looked—in clothes we'd worn since early morning and without so much as having washed our faces all day. And Eddie and Isabel, who wouldn't have dreamed of going to the theater that way in Houston, were ready to do it in London.

The whole thing was academic for me: I couldn't have stood on that line for ten minutes, much less an hour. I'd stood peering in at shop windows most of the day with my teeth gritted and by six I'd had it. I told them I thought I'd call it a day and go sit somewhere before my insides fell out on the pavement. They're old friends, they immediately abandoned the project and we went to dinner at a little side-street pub instead.

Not till I got home did it dawn on me that they and I had completely reversed roles. Coming abroad, where nobody knows them, Eddie and Isabel have rid themselves of a lot of social inhibitions. Coming abroad, where noboddy knows me, I've acquired a whole set of inhibitions I never had at home. Wild?

Carmen just phoned to remind me of the Autograph Party tomorrow and the Deutsch dinner tomorrow night. I told her I have a calendar propped against the traveling clock so it's the first thing I see when I turn the alarm off in the morning.

Asked her what I do if nobody shows up for my autograph; she said briskly Talk to the manager, he's a fan. After twenty minutes say you have a headache and he'll get you a cab.

We toured the bookshops in the rain. They all had *84* prominently displayed, and all the managers and sales people bowed and beamed and shook my hand, and after the third bookshop I got terribly poised and gracious about it all, like I was used to it. We got to Poole's at two-thirty for the Autograph Party—and would you believe a long line of people waiting for my important autograph? On a rainy Tuesday?

They'd set up a table for me at the head of the line and I sat down and asked the first man to tell me his name and a bit about himself so I could write something personal, I can*not* break myself of the habit of autographing books with chummy little messages that take up the whole front page.

A lady from California plunked down twelve copies and got out her list and said, This first one's for her brother Arnold in the hospital, could I write something cheerful? and this one's for Mrs. Pratt next door who's watering her plants, and this one's for her daughter-in-law Pat, could I write "To Pat From Mother Crawford Via—"? Twelve. Now and then I'd squint along the line (I wasn't wearing my glasses, I'm a celebrity) and apologize for keeping everybody waiting; they all just smiled and went on standing patiently, people are unbelievable.

I got nearly to the end of the line and said automatically without looking up, "Will you tell me your name, sir?" and he said "Pat Buckley," meekly, and I looked up and there he was with two books under his arms. I told him I want to give him a copy. I autographed his two for him to give to friends.

He asked whether I'm free on Saturday if he's "able to arrange a little outing"; I said I'm free for any outing he arranges any day at all, and he beamed and said he'd be in touch.

After the autographing, I had sherry with the manager, Mr. Port. (Fact.) He gave me a letter someone had left there for me and I put it in my shoulder bag and brought it home and just now remembered it and got it out and opened it.

Dear Miss Hanff—

Welcome to England. A benefactor from Philadelphia sent us your book and we love it, as do all our friends.

I wonder if you would be free on Monday next, June 28, and would like to see Peter Brook's production of "A Midsummer Night's Dream" with us? It is at the National Shakespeare Company's London theater, the Aldwych. We are taking two Australian friends with us, both devotees of your book.

My husband is English, so am I, but I had an American mother.

We'd love it if you are free to come. Will you telephone me?—and we can plan where to meet and eat first.

Sincerely,

Joyce Grenfell

I feel as if God had leaned down from heaven and pasted a gold star on my forehead.

I'm sitting here all gussied up in the silk cocktail-dress-and-coat for the Deutsch dinner, ready half an hour early as usual. I'm afraid even to smoke, I'll get ashes on it.

*1 a.m.*

The desk buzzed up when the car came, and when I went down to the lobby, Mr. Otto, the Kenilworth manager, bowed ceremoniously and said:

"Madam's car awaits."

Told him this was my first and last chance to be a celebrity and I was gonna make the most of it. He nodded solemnly and said: "Quite." He and the two boys who work as desk clerks get a charge out of all my roses and phone calls and notes-left-at-the-desk. So do I, believe it.

The dinner party was at a Hungarian restaurant called Victor's. Victor is a close friend of André Deutsch, they're both Hungarian but Victor is more so. He bowed and kissed my hand and told me I was "beautiful" and "Queen of London for a month" and my book was also "beautiful." I told Deutsch:

"He's straight out of Molnar."

And Deutsch looked at me in mild surprise and said:

"Oh, did you know Ferenc?"

No, I didn't know Ferenc but Deutsch did. If any Molnar fan is still alive and reading this, you pronounce it Ference.

The dinner was in a private upstairs dining room; we paraded up the carpeted stairs, about eight of us, and into a dining room, where a large round table was just jumping with wine glasses and flowers and candles. I sat between Deutsch, very old-world and courtly, and the "distinguished journalist" whose name I didn't get.

Everybody at dinner was bowled over to learn I was going to meet Joyce Grenfell. I know her as a comedienne in British films but she's much more famous over here for her one-man shows, which I never saw. She writes all her own material and the show always sells out. So now of course I'm nervous about meeting her.

Over coffee, somebody passed a copy of *84* around the table for all the guests to sign for me. Above the signatures somebody had written a flowery tribute to "an author who combines talent with charm" and sociability with something else, and Deutsch read it and nodded vehemently and signed his name and handed the book to me with a flourish. And Victor read it and said Yes, Yes, it was So! and signed his name ("Your host!") and kissed my hand again, and dessert was a fancy decorated cake with WELCOME HELENE on it in pink icing.

Got home at midnight, swept into the lobby and informed Mr. Otto and the boys at the desk I am hereafter to be known as the Duchess of Bloomsbury. Or Bloomsbury Street, at least.

The two desk clerks are students from South Africa. One of them has to go back in a few days, and the other advised him conversationally:

"If the police come after you, eat my address."

Nora and I were taken to lunch by a rare-book dealer, and over lunch a bizarre story from Nora.

I gather book dealers are as clannish as actors, and the closest friends Frank and Nora had for ten years were a book dealer named Peter Kroger and his wife, Helen. The Doels and Krogers were inseparable despite the fact that the two men were competitors. One New Year's Eve, the Doels gave a party, and Helen Kroger arrived looking very exotic in a long black evening dress.

"Helen, you look like a Russian spy!" said Nora. And Helen laughed and Peter laughed and a few months later Nora picked up the morning paper and discovered that Helen and Peter Kroger *were* Russian spies.

"All the journalists came swarming round to the house," Nora told me, "offering me a couple of thousand quid to tell them about 'the ring.' I told them the only ring I knew anything about was my wedding ring."

She visited the Krogers in prison and Peter asked if she remembered telling Helen she looked like a Russian spy.

"It must have given them a turn," I said.

"I don't know," said Nora. "He just asked if I remembered it. Then we talked about something else."

She and Frank went to the trial and discovered that everything the Krogers had told them about their past lives had been invented. I asked if this bothered her, Nora said No, she understood it.

"They were the best friends we ever had," she said. "They were fine people, lovely people. It was all political, I s'pose they had their reasons."

A year later the Krogers were exchanged for a British spy held by the Russians. They live in Poland now. Helen and Nora still write to each other at Christmas.

Phoned Joyce Grenfell at dinner time, told her what movies I'd seen her in and she said:

"Then you'll know me, I'm the one with the bangs." I'm to meet them for dinner Monday at the Waldorf, which is next door to the theater.

*Thursday, June 24*

I finally got a day to myself and did the Regent's Park area on foot. Walked around the Nash Crescent twenty or thirty times, saw the house on Wimpole Street where Robert Browning came to call on Elizabeth, walked Harley Street—and also Devonshire Street, Devonshire Place, Devonshire Mews, Devonshire Close and Devonshire Mews Close, this is a lovely city.

There was a note at the desk for me when I came back. No salutation.

> Can you be here at twelve noon *sharp* on Saturday? We are driving down to Windsor and Eton and have rather a lot to do.
>
> In haste—
>
> P.B.

We are driving down to Windsor and Eton. Me, this is.

I love the way he never uses a salutation. It always aggravates me, when I'm writing to some telephone-company supervisor or insurance man, to have to begin with "Dear Sir" when he and I both know nobody on earth is less dear to me.

I'm writing this in the Kenilworth Lounge. Not to be confused with the Kenilworth TV Room, where everybody sits bolt upright on little straight chairs in total darkness staring at some situation comedy. The Lounge is just off the lobby. It's a pleasant room with easy chairs and a sofa, but

if you want to write in your journal you have to slither an
eye around the door before entering. If there's a woman
alone in here she's looking for somebody to talk to. If there
are two women already talking, they're gracious and friendly
enough to include you in the conversation, and you can't
decline to be included without seeming *un*gracious and
*un*friendly.

Tonight when I came in there was only a man at the
desk writing letters, he just left. He asked me for a light,
and when he heard my American accent he told me he'd
lived in New York for a year.

"And then one day I was walking down Fifth Avenue
with an American friend and I said to him: 'Why are you
running?' And he said: 'I'm not running!' And then I knew
it was time to come home."

People here ask you for "a light" only if you're smoking
and they can light their cigarette from yours. Nobody would
dream of asking you for a match, it would be like asking you
for money. Matches are not free over here. There are none in
ashtrays in hotel lobbies and none on restaurant tables. You
have to buy them at the store, I suppose they're imported
and too expensive to fling around the way they're flung
around at home.

A lady just came in, she asked Am I the writer? she
heard about me at the desk. She lives in Kent, she doesn't
care for London, she's here because her brother's in the
hospital here but at least she's seeing a bit of Bloomsbury, he
just won't hear of her staying in the room all day, so this
afternoon she went out to the Dickens House in Doughty
Street, have I been there?

She wants to talk so we'll talk.

---

I got the first week's hotel bill this morning, much steeper than I'd anticipated, what with assorted lunches and dinners and a 12 per cent surcharge added for tips. I just took it up the street to Deutsch's, to Mr. Tammer, their accountant. He's a solemn, bespectacled gentleman who gives you a sudden warm smile when you say hello to him. He's got all my "advance" money in cash in the office safe and he's doling it out to me weekly. He gave me cash to pay the hotel bill and ten pounds, which is my Allowance for the week; when I run short I dip into my brother's hundred. I had ten of the hundred with me for him to change into pounds, and he got out all his charts and machines and figured the latest exchange rate very tensely and meticulously, God forbid he should cheat me out of fifteen cents.

There was a letter for me at Deutsch's which intrigues me, it's from a man I never knew existed. Nobody I corresponded with at Marks & Co. ever mentioned him.

Dear Miss Hanff,

I am the son of the late Ben Marks of Marks & Co. and want you to know how delighted I am that you are here, and how very much my wife and I would like you to dine with us.

I do not know where you are staying so could you please ring me at the above telephone numbers? The second one is an answering service and any message left there will reach me.

We're both looking forward to meeting you.

Sincerely,

Leo Marks

The secretary who gave me the letter told me he called and asked where he could reach me.

"But we never tell anyone where you're staying," she said. "We just ask them to get in touch with you through us."

I took a very dim view of this and went into Carmen's office to straighten it out.

"Carmen, dear," I said, "I am not the kind of author who wants to be protected from her public. Any fan who phones might want to feed me, and I am totally available as a dinner guest. Just give out my address all over."

She said there are at least two interviews to come and she'll make them both over lunch. Some interviewer asked me if I planned "to buy silver and cashmere here—or just books?" I said I planned to buy *nothing* over here, everything I see in a shop window has a price tag reading "One Day Less in London."

Off to Parliament.

*Midnight*

I'VE BEEN TO THE OLD VIC, shades of my stage-struck youth, walking into that theater was a thrill. Nora and

Sheila and I saw *Mrs. Warren's Profession*. The theater has the atmosphere of the old Met in New York and the Academy of Music in Philadelphia; the audience files in with a kind of festive reverence, like people going to church on Christmas Eve.

Sheila had trouble parking the car, she got to the theater three minutes after the curtain was up and was promptly shunted off downstairs to the lounge to watch the first act on closed-circuit TV, you do not trail down the aisle after Mass has started.

I'll never understand why they did *Mrs. Warren's Profession* in turn-of-the-century costumes. Politicians and businessmen don't own whorehouses any more? Poor girls are not expected to starve virtuously rather than eat unvirtuously any more? Moral pillars of society don't keep mistresses in country cottages any more? Who does such a play as a costume piece belonging to some other era? Bernie Shaw would have a fit.

I asked Nora about Leo Marks, she said she only met him and his wife a few times but "they seemed a nice young couple." She said he's a writer.

I'm sitting here eating vitamin C, think I'm getting a cold. Tried reading Mary Baker Eddy once, should've stuck with it.

It finally turned sunny and warm, thank God, so I could wear a skirt for PB. (Headline in the newspaper read ENGLAND SWELTERS IN 75-DEGREE HEAT.) Wore my brown linen skirt and the new white blazer, and he beamed and said, "You look charming," and asked if the brown-and-white scarf came from Harrods. (I borrowed it off the cocktail dress.)

He said as we drove that we wouldn't be able to go through Windsor Castle after all, "the Queen's in residence," but we would stop at Windsor for sherry with two elderly sisters, he thought I'd find them and their house delightful.

On the way to Windsor there's a Home for Tired Horses. Their owners visit them on Sundays and bring them cream buns.

Windsor is full of casual anachronisms. The sisters live on a seventeenth-century street in one of a row of Queen Anne houses, each with a car parked at the curb and a TV antenna sticking out of the roof. PB parked at the back of the house by the rose garden and we were met there by the dominant sister, who cut a pink rose for me to wear and took us into the house and along a narrow old-fashioned hall to the living room, where the shy sister met us. The shy sister poured sherry and both of them regretfully informed PB that their ghost had gone.

The ghost was living in the house when they bought it twenty years ago and he stayed on. He was very quiet and no trouble most of the time. But he liked the house to be lived in, he liked people about; and every time the sisters packed up for a trip and made arrangements to close the house, the ghost went berserk with fury. Pictures were knocked off the walls, wine glasses went hurtling off the sideboard and broke, lamps crashed to the floor, pots and pans went clattering and banging round the kitchen all night long. The rampage lasted till the sisters left for their holiday. For twenty years, this happened every time they went up to London during the season or into the country or abroad. This year, for the first time, the sisters made plans to go away, they packed for the trip—and the house remained silent. The pictures and wine glasses and lamps were undisturbed, the kitchen was quiet, the ghost had gone. The sisters were rather sad about it, they'd got fond of him.

One of the sisters took me up to the top-floor bathroom to look out the window. They run up there to see whether the Queen has arrived. From the bathroom window you can see the Windsor Castle flagpole. If the Queen's in residence the flag is flying.

They apologized for not giving us lunch, they were going to watch Philip play polo.

PB and I picnicked on the Windsor lawn. He (or the daily) had packed a basket with three kinds of sandwiches, a thermos of iced tea, peaches and cookies—and after-dinner mints, I love him to death, there's an Edwardian finishing touch to everything he does. Like the china ashtray he keeps on the front ledge of his car, he obviously doesn't care for the tin one that comes built in.

There's a footbridge connecting Windsor and Eton. PB wore his Eton tie, and the gate keeper saw it and said, "You're an Eton man, sir!" and let us into rooms not open to tourists.

If you're born in the U.S. with a yearning love of classical scholarship and no college education, you are awed by a school in which for centuries boys have learned to read and write Greek and Latin fluently by the time they're in their teens. PB took me into the original classroom, five hundred years old, and made me sit at one of the desks. They're dark, heavy oak, thickly covered with boys' initials scratched into the wood with pocket knives. Five hundred years' worth of boys' initials is something to see.

We went into the chapel where the senior boys worship, there's a roll book hanging from the aisle pew of each row so that every boy's presence can be checked off by a monitor. We read the names in one—"Harris Major. Harris Minor. Harris Tertius"—Eton never does in English what it can do in Latin.

Along the hall outside the classrooms the high oak walls have names cut into them as thickly as the initials in the desks. PB told me when a boy graduates he pays a few shillings to the college to have his name carved in the wall. We saw Pitt's name and Shelley's (and PB showed me his own). You could spend a month crawling up and down the walls looking for names.

Heart-rending plaques to Eton's war dead. One family lost eight men in World War I, seven of them in their twenties. The Grenfells (Joyce Grenfell's husband's family) lost grandfather, father and one son—and six men in the Boer War a dozen years earlier.

We went outside and saw the playing fields where all those wars were supposedly won. Boys were playing cricket, a few strolled by swinging tennis rackets. On Saturdays the boys are allowed to wear ordinary sports clothes but we saw several in the Eton uniform: black tail coat, white shirt, striped trousers. PB says they don't wear the top hat any more except on state occasions. (Those top hats kept the boys out of trouble. If an Eton boy tried to sneak into an off-limits pub or movie, the manager could spot that top hat from anywhere in the house and throw him out.)

The faces of the boys are unbelievably clean and chiseled and beautiful. And the tail coats—which must have looked outlandish in the 1940's and 50's—look marvelously appropriate with the long hair the boys wear now. What with the cameo faces, the long hair brushed to a gleam and perfectly cut tails, they looked like improbable Edwardian princes.

We drove back to London at four; PB wanted to take me through Marlborough House and it closes at five. We drove to Marlborough House but couldn't go through it, the guard explained the house is closed for cleaning. The Royal Chapel is open, and PB told me to go to services there one Sunday. He said it's never crowded or touristy since few people know it's open to the public. Queen Mary was married there, so I'm going, out of affection for her and Pope-Hennessy.

*Later*

Laura Davidson just phoned from Oxford. She wrote me a fan letter telling me her husband, a Swarthmore professor, was working at Balliol for a year and that they and their fifteen-year-old son were fans of the book and wanted me to come to Oxford. I wrote back and told her when I was coming to London and she actually rescheduled a Paris vacation just so she'd be in Oxford when I came. When I picked up the phone just now and said hello, she said:

"Hi, it's Laura Davidson, how are you, when are you coming to Oxford? My son is dying of suspense."

We settled on next Friday. She said there are trains almost every hour, call and let her know which one I'm on and she'll meet it. She'll carry the book so I'll know her.

I'm paranoid enough about traveling when I'm home and healthy, and the prospect of strange railroad stations and train trips over here kind of wears me out. But Oxford I have to see. There's one suite of freshman's rooms at Trinity College which John Donne, John Henry Newman and Arthur Quiller-Couch all lived in, in various long-gone eras. Whatever I know about writing English those three men taught me, and before I die I want to stand in their freshman's rooms and call their names blessed.

Q (Quiller-Couch) was all by himself my college education. I went down to the public library one day when I was seventeen looking for books on the art of writing, and found five books of lectures which Q had delivered to his students of writing at Cambridge.

"Just what I need!" I congratulated myself. I hurried

home with the first volume and started reading and got to page 3 and hit a snag:

Q was lecturing to young men educated at Eton and Harrow. He therefore assumed that his students—including me—had read *Paradise Lost* as a matter of course and would understand his analysis of the "Invocation to Light" in Book 9. So I said, "Wait here," and went down to the library and got *Paradise Lost* and took it home and started reading it and got to page 3, when I hit a snag:

Milton assumed I'd read the Christian version of Isaiah and the New Testament and had learned all about Lucifer and the War in Heaven, and since I'd been reared in Judaism I hadn't. So I said, "Wait here," and borrowed a Christian Bible and read about Lucifer and so forth, and then went back to Milton and read *Paradise Lost,* and then finally got back to Q, page 3. On page 4 or 5, I discovered that the point of the sentence at the top of the page was in Latin and the long quotation at the bottom of the page was in Greek. So I advertised in the *Saturday Review* for somebody to teach me Latin and Greek, and went back to Q meanwhile, and discovered he assumed I not only knew all the plays of Shakespeare, and Boswell's *Johnson,* but also the Second book of Esdras, which is not in the Old Testament and not in the New Testament, it's in the Apocrypha, which is a set of books nobody had ever thought to tell me existed.

So what with one thing and another and an average of three "Wait here's" a week, it took me eleven years to get through Q's five books of lectures.

Q also introduced me to John Henry Newman, who taught at Oriel, Oxford, and when I finish with Trinity I'm going over to Oriel and sit in John Henry's chapel and tell him I still don't know what he was talking about most of the time but I've got whole pages of the *Apologia* by heart, and I own a first edition of *The Idea of a University*.

PB is right, the Royal Chapel at Marlborough is not at all touristy and few people know it's open to the public. If it is.

I dressed very carefully and went down there this morning. Only a handful of people attended the service. All of them obviously worship there every Sunday, all of them obviously know each other and all of them spent most of the service trying to figure out who I was. From the whispers and sidelong glances you could reconstruct the dialogue:

"My dear, don't look now . . ."

". . . back there on the end pew, a few rows behind . . ."

*Bzz-bzz-bzz.*

One angular, elderly lady got out her spectacles just to have a good long squint at me. Then she turned to the wispy friend sitting next to her and shook her head "No!" firmly. The wispy lady refused to be daunted. She kept staring at me with the tentative half-smile you use when you know the face but just can't place it. I made the mistake of smiling back, and from then on neither of them took their eyes off me.

I was also the only shoulder bag in the house, if I have to add that.

At the end of the service I was the first one up the aisle and out of there.

Had to come back up here for lunch. NOTHING is open here on Sunday, you could starve.

I'm lying under a tree in St. James's Park. There are three downtown parks adjoining each other—St. James's and Green, both small, and the big one, Hyde Park.

All the parks here are very serene, very gentle. Young couples go by, arm in arm, quietly, no transistor radios or guitars in hand. Families picnic on the lawn sedately. Dogs go by on leashes, equally sedate, looking neither to the right nor to the left. There was one exception: a woman came by with a small gray poodle on a leash, I said hello to the poodle and he veered toward me, always-glad-to-meet-a-friend, but the woman yanked him back.

"Please don't do that!" she said to me sharply. "I'm trying to teach him good manners."

I thought, " A pity he can't do the same for you," and had a sudden vision of Dog Hill on a Sunday afternoon and wondered how everybody was.

We had a picnic there one night—Dick, who lives in my building and owns an English sheep dog, and my friend Nikki and I. I had some cold turkey for sandwiches and I deviled some eggs, and Dick made a thermos of bloody marys and we went over to the hill with Chester-the-Sheep-Dog. Nikki came up from her office and met us there. You have to be crazy to picnic on Dog Hill, but Dick and I thought we'd try it. We didn't get there till six-thirty, most of the dogs had gone home.

Dog Hill is a broad, sloping hill in Central Park, and the largest canine Social Hall in the world. On a weekend afternoon you'll see forty or fifty dogs up there, charging around off leash meeting friends. (You don't take a dog to

Dog Hill unless he's a friend to the world but I never met a New York dog who wasn't.) On a good day you'll see everything from Afghans and Norwegian elkhounds to Shih-tzus and Lhasa Apsos, not to mention all the standard brands. The dog owners sit on the grass or stand around like parents at a children's party, keeping an eye out for sudden spats over whose stick it is or whose ball it is.

"George, if you can't play nicely we're going home!"

"Mabel, get off him! I don't wanna hear about it, just get off him!"

You do not stretch out on the grass to sunbathe because if a couple of great Danes and a collie are having a race and you're lying in their path they're not going to detour for you.

Dick and Nikki and I settled at the top of the hill and Dick poured out the bloody marys in paper cups. A few dogs were playing halfway down the hill, and normally Chester-the-Sheep-Dog would have joined them. But he'd smelled the picnic basket all the way to the park so he just loped down the hill and sniffed everybody and then came back up, figuring he'd hang around us till dinner time.

I understood this, so when I got out the sandwiches I gave Chester a sliver of turkey out of mine. That was all it took. In five seconds, there was a semicircle of dogs in front of me: every dog left on the hill had come to the picnic.

There were two basset-hound brothers named Sam and Sid, Romulus, who is a great Dane, a beagle I didn't know and a very timid German shepherd pup named Helga—all standing stock still, eyes glued to me and my turkey sandwich. The beagle was drooling.

I had an extra sandwich in reserve so I sacrificed the

one I'd started on and gave each dog in turn a sliver of turkey. (Helga was very nervous, she was anxious to step up for her piece of turkey but how did she know I wouldn't bite her?)

Chester-the-Sheep-Dog figured there was too much competition, so he left and trotted back to visit Nikki's sandwich. And just as I was feeding the rest of the dogs the last of the turkey, Nikki set up a great to-do because Chester had taken a sip of her bloody mary. Dick called, "Chester! Sit!" And Chester, wanting to show how well-trained he was, sat on Nikki's deviled egg. Whereupon Nikki took a fit. (She's young and pretty and she went to the London School of Economics for a year, but she's a cat lover.) I turned and called Chester, hoping to lure him away from her—and the instant my back was turned, the beagle (Morton, I think his name was) seized the untouched reserve sandwich and made off down the hill with it.

His mother came up to apologize and thank me; she said he only eats chicken and now she wouldn't have to cook for him when they got home.

We walked back down through the park to the Seventy-second Street entrance, past a baseball game and an impromptu marimba band fighting a rock concert that penetrated clear up from Fifty-ninth street.

Lying in peaceful St. James's, I realize how much a city's parks reflect the character of its people. The parks here are tranquil, quiet, a bit reserved, and I love them. But on a long-term basis, I would sorely miss the noisy exuberance of Central Park.

*9 p.m.*

The Colonel phoned up, he's back. He said, What part of our glorious countryside did I want to see most? I told him I was going to Oxford next Friday and I'd be very grateful if he wanted to drive me there.

"Well, now!" he boomed. "We can do much better than that, my dear! If you're free on Thursday, we can drive through the Cotswolds and be in Stratford-on-Avon in time for dinner and the theater, and drive on to meet your friends in Oxford on Friday."

I was wildly excited, which surprised me. I'm not terribly attracted to birthplaces, to me Shakespeare was born in the Globe Theater. But when he said he was taking me to Stratford-on-Avon I shouted my excitement, you can't help it.

Asked if he knew a shop where I could buy a cheap overnight bag and he said:

"Nonsense, I'll send a nice BOAC bag round to you."

I tell you it's insidious being an ersatz Duchess, people rushing to give you what you want before you've had time to want it. If I kept this up for more than a month it would ruin my moral fiber.

I'd left my number with Leo Marks's answering service and he called back this morning. He has a beautiful Oxford baritone. (Or Cambridge. I don't know the difference.) He and his wife will pick me up for dinner tomorrow night at seven.

Dinner and *Midsummer Night* with the Grenfells tonight, so this morning I took my cocktail dress downstairs and said to the young desk clerk:

"Can I have this pressed before five this evening?"

"D'you want it cleaned or laundered?" he asked.

"No, just pressed," I said.

He stared at me blankly.

"Do you want it sent to the Cleaner's?" he repeated, emphasizing each word as carefully as if I were Russian or deaf, "or do you want it sent to the Laundry?"

"I don't want it cleaned *or* washed," I said, enunciating as carefully as if *he* were Russian or deaf, "I just want it *pressed*. It's *wrinkled*."

This seemed to stun him. He stared at me a moment. Then he pulled himself together, mumbled, "Scuse me," and went off to consult the Office. In a minute he was back.

"If you'll go up to Room 315 and speak to the housekeeper," he said, "p'raps she can help you."

I went up and knocked on the door of Room 315 and explained my problem to the motherly-looking housekeeper. She nodded understandingly and said, "Come this way, dear," and led me down to the end of the hall and opened the door to a little dungeon with an ironing board and an ancient monster iron in one corner.

---

"You can press it right here, dear," she said. "Mind the iron, the cord's a bit frayed."

I was a bit frayed myself by this time. The dress is silk, the iron was unfamiliar and didn't look friendly. I took the dress down to the desk and told the clerk to send it to the Cleaner's, he was very relieved. This is what comes of being allergic to chemical fabrics in a drip-dry world.

*Later*

I got lost trying to find the Waldorf on foot, overshot it by two blocks, ran back and tore into the lobby ten minutes late—and Joyce Grenfell must have been watching the door, she came out to meet me looking exactly as she looks on the screen.

She led the way into the dining room and introduced me to her husband—"RegGEE!" she mostly calls him—and their Australian friends, Sir Charles and Lady Fitts, he's a famous doctor. I sat down, suddenly shaken by the fact that these four distinguished people had wanted to meet *me*. I tell you, life is extraordinary. A few years ago I couldn't write anything or sell anything, I'd passed the age where you know all the returns are in, I'd had my chance and done my best and failed. And how was I to know the miracle waiting to happen round the corner in late middle age? *84, Charing Cross Road* was no best seller, you understand; it didn't make me rich or famous. It just got me hundreds of letters and phone calls from people I never knew existed; it got me wonderful reviews; it restored a self-confidence and self-esteem I'd lost somewhere along the way, God knows how many years ago. It brought me to England. It changed my life.

The Grenfells had got house seats for themselves and the Australians, and when Joyce read I was in town she invited me along—even though it meant Reggie had to give up his house seat to me and go sit in the balcony, I was horrified.

It's an experience walking down a theater aisle with a famous theater personality. Every eye in the audience was on her, and when we took our seats you could feel necks craning all over the house.

Peter Brook's production initially a shock, half play, half noisy circus. Mrs. G. was immediately entranced; I kept worrying about whether Puck was going to fall off his stilts or drop the plates he was juggling. Halfway through the second act I was suddenly moved, and I thought, "I resent it but I love it." Stimulates you to death, seeing Shakespeare explode all over a stage like that.

They drove me home after saying goodbye to the Australians. Joyce drove because it's a new car and Reggie wanted her to get the feel of it.

She had a hell of a time in Bloomsbury. The one-way streets here set drivers crazy, you have to go five blocks out of your way to find a street going in the right direction. And she was NOT going to drop me across Shaftsbury Avenue on the wrong corner of Great Russell Street, she would NOT drop me round the corner on Bloomsbury Street, the hotel entrance was on Great Russell and she was By God going to drop me in front of the door. And after zigzagging north and south for half an hour she triumphantly did it and accepted my congratulations graciously.

She said they're "going on holiday" but will be back on July 13 for her church dialogue. She has a monthly church dialogue with a minister—on The Nature of Love and The Nature of Beauty and so forth—at a noon service at St. Mary LaBeau's Church in Cheapside. She said Why don't I come to the July 13 dialogue and then come to dinner that night and they'll drive me around to see the sights. I told her I wasn't certain I'd still be here on the thirteenth, though I'm hoping to last till the fifteenth.

During the second act, that cold caught up with me. I started to cough and nearly strangled trying to muffle it. I leaned over and whispered to Joyce apologetically:

"I've been fighting a cold all weekend."

She thought about this a moment and then leaned over and whispered back:

"Oh, have it."

So I'm having it. Sitting up in bed hacking and snuffling and even that doesn't depress me. I seem to be living in a state of deep hypnosis, every time I mail a postcard home I could use Euphoria for a return address.

I'm in the dining room having my fourth or fifth cup of coffee, feeling the way you feel the first morning of a full-blown cold. I was going to call Leo Marks and cancel dinner but if I stay in the hotel all day I'll want to get out of it tonight so I'll keep the date and try not to cough in their faces.

The dining room's emptying out now; between eight and nine every morning it's jammed and the waiters are frantic. The room rate here includes "Full English Breakfast" and we all eat everything: fruit juice or cereal, bacon and eggs, toast and marmalade, tea or coffee (and the girl who brings the coffee pot asks "Black or white?").

The breakfast regulars always include British Willie Lomans in from the country on business and a sprinkling of middle-aged women from all over "the U.K." traveling alone. (They never say "Great Britain," it's "the U.K."— United Kingdom.) Several pale, pointy-nosed professors are stowing away enough fuel to last them through the day at the British museum, they all look as if they lunch on yogurt.

This morning, a long table of Scots matrons here for a conference accompanied by a scrubbed young vicar. Ladies all complained they didn't sleep a *wink* for the noise, the motorcars go by in the street just-all-NIGHT. Quietest place I ever slept in. They should try tucking up over Second Avenue, where the trucks start rolling at 3 A.M.

Lots of Russian and Czech tourist families here, with blasé well-behaved children. Several parties of German tourists, middle-aged to make it worse. (The young ones you don't mind: they-didn't-do-it.) The tourist parties all eat with one eye on the clock; they've all signed up for some bus tour and the buses leave the hotel at nine sharp. At two minutes to nine there's a heavy Russian-Czech-German bustle and a ponderous exodus to the line—where the Czechs gesticulate wildly at signs they can't read and the German tour leader bawls, *"Achtung!"* and, *"Halte!"* to get everybody lined up. The Russians just stolidly find the bus and get on it.

The only Americans here besides me turned up at breakfast this morning for the first time: three California college girls, blond, tanned, radiantly healthy, conferring anxiously on whether Full English Breakfast meant you could order everything, it's all free with the room? I asked the waitress for more coffee and when they heard my American accent one of them came over to my table to ask about what you can order and Are you supposed to tip. I said No, the management adds 12 per cent to your bill for tips. Alvaro was scandalized when I tried to tip him the first day. No, No! he said, It is all cared for!

Will now retire to my room with last weekend's newspapers and their fiendish crossword puzzles and spend the morning "enjoying poor health," as my mother used to say.

### Crime Note

From Saturday's evening paper:

£50 FINE FOR TEACHER
WHO ASSAULTED GIRL
AT WIMBLEDON

A 54-year-old teacher of statistics at London University . . . appeared in court today charged with insulting behavior at Wimbledon tennis championships.

He was fined £50 after admitting indecent assault in the standing area of No. 1 Court.

Temporary Det. Con. Patrick Doyle told Wimbledon magistrates that [the defendant] put an arm around an 18-year-old girl and held her breasts.

[The defendant], who is married, said:

"I suffered a temporary lapse of commonsense.

"It is ridiculous that a man in my position should do such a thing."

A Wimbledon umpire . . . aged 66, was also accused of insulting behavior at Wimbledon. Altogether 10 men appeared, charged with insulting behavior.

The sixty-year-old umpire was extra lucky, they put his picture in the paper.

Here's a help-wanted ad for you:

---

BUCKINGHAM PALACE. Vacancy in the central wash-up of the main kitchen, for female applicants only. Non-residential. . . . Apply in writing to Master of the Household, Buckingham Palace, London SW 1

---

Wouldn't you like to take that job for one day, just to listen to the gossip?

*11 p.m.*

Leo Marks phoned up from the lobby at seven, I went down to meet them in my silk-dress-and-coat, red nose and watery eyes, and Leo, who is dark-haired and good-looking, said:

"How d'you do, we're very glad you could come, go back upstairs and get a coat, it's chilly and it's raining."

I came up and got my old blue coat, went down and told him:

"You've made me ruin the effect of my whole costume."

And Ena—his wife, very small and blond—said earnestly:

"You can take the coat off when we get to the restaurant, we're dining at a hotel, you can take it off in the lobby!" and peered at me anxiously to see if that was all right.

She ought to look delicate but doesn't, you get a sense of wiry strength. She might be a small blond athlete but she's a portrait painter. She paints under her own name, Ena Gaussen. Leo told me she's done portraits of Hayley Mills and Pamela Brown and won all sorts of citations; she doesn't look old enough.

They took me to the Stafford, a very old, gracious hotel rather like the Plaza. I had a couple of martinis to clear the sinuses and discovered Leo is a gin drinker. He's also a TV and film writer and we found we'd worked for the same TV producer—in different seasons and on different continents—and we talked shop. Ena didn't mind, she thinks we're both terribly witty.

He calls her "little thing."

"Little thing, you want the lobster again?"

He asked me if I knew of the pianist Eileen Joyce and told me:

"She's just been made a Dame of the British Empire and she wants the little thing to paint her in her Dame's robes."

When it was too late to go see it, Ena told me one of Leo's films was playing around the corner; I was very impressed. I've always believed film writing is the most difficult form a writer can work in.

"Tell me," said Leo. "You've written a beautiful book. Why haven't we heard from you before? What was wrong with your earlier work? Too good or not good enough."

"Not good enough," I said. And he nodded and went on to something else, and I think that's when we became soul mates.

It was a marvelous evening. I'd love to see them again but I haven't the nerve to call and suggest it. Being a visiting fireman has its own courtesy rules.

cough-cough-cough-cough-cough.

Being a celebrity means you're paged to the phone three times during breakfast, and the first time you come back to the table your eggs are cold, the second time you come back your eggs are GONE and the third time you carry a fresh plate of eggs out to the lobby phone with you.

Joyce Grenfell phoned to ask how my cough was and to say Do-be-here-on-the-thirteenth. I told her I mean to. The hotel switchboard operator recognized her voice and didn't put the call through to the booth, I took it at the desk, and the switchboard operator and cashier both like to collapse when I held the receiver out so they could hear her call, "RegGEEE!" when she wanted to ask him something.

Nora phoned and heard my croak and said Why didn't I come out to North London and let her nurse me? That's all she needs; she's working at a full-time job since Frank died.

The Colonel phoned to say the BOAC bag "will be sent round this A.M." and he'll pick me up at ten tomorrow morning for the trip to Stratford-and-Oxford.

After breakfast I went across the street for Kleenex and cough drops. There's a string of small stores opposite the hotel on Great Russell Street: a stationery store, a Unisex Beauty Shop, a Cinema Bookshop and an Indian food store that carries health-food items. There's also a large YWCA Women's Residence and a curbside fruit stand. I stopped at the fruit stand for some peaches, and while I was waiting for change I noticed a bulletin board in a glass case outside the stationery store. Got my change and went over to read the bulletin board. At first glance the notices seem to be Items-for-Sale and Situations-Wanted ads, but you don't have to read very far to discover your mistake. To the pure in heart, however, all bulletin boards are pure, viz.: (This is the entire bulletin-board list.)

---

Hot Pants for sale. Phone . . . . . . . . . . . . . . . . . . . . . . .

———

Ex-actress will give lessons. French or anything. Phone . . . . . . . . . . . . . . . . . . . . . . . . . . . . . . . . . . . . . . . . . . . . . . .

———

Male model. All services. TV, photog, rubber, leather. Corrective training. Phone . . . . . . . . . . . . . . . . . . . . . .

———

Model seeks unusual positions. Miss Coucher. Phone . . . . . . . . . . . . . . . . . . . . . . . . . . . . . . . . . . . . . . . . . . . . . . . . .

———

New lovely blonde doll for sale. Walks, talks. Phone . . . . . . . . . . . . . . . . . . . . . . . . . . . . . . . . . . . . . . . . . . . . . . . .

———

Tom Tamer gives lessons in the most strict deportment. Phone . . . . . . . . . . . . . . . . . . . . . . . . . . . . . . . . . . . . . . .

———

French girl. Ex-governess, many positions. Seeks new pupils. Both sexes. Phone . . . . . . . . . . . . . . . . . . . . . .

———

Three rucksacks wanted. Good condition. Reasonable. Contact YWCA, Great Russell St.

---

*7 p.m.*

Ena blew in at five-thirty with a brown paper bag full of lemons, honey and lime juice for my cough. She said she had an urge all morning to call me and hang on the phone but felt shy about it; I said we're both too inhibited. She wanted me to have dinner with them tomorrow night. I told her I'd be in Stratford but would be back Friday, and her face fell.

"We go down to the country on Friday and we won't be back until the tenth!" she said.

"Never mind," I said. "I have every intention of lasting till the fifteenth."

She looked distressed.

"You can't go home that soon! We've only just met you!" she said. "Look, when you run out of money why don't you go down and stay at our place in the country? We shan't be using it at all after the tenth, you could stay there all summer—if you don't mind our coming down weekends?" peering at me anxiously. People unhinge me.

She just left to meet Leo at his mother's.

The BOAC bag arrived, and I phoned the Colonel and thanked him. He advised me to eat a lot:

"You must always feed a cold. If you don't give the germs food to eat they'll feed on you."

Will now go down to the dining room and feed the germs.

*Later*

I ordered "Chicken Maryland," which turned out to be a slice of chicken, breaded and fried flat like a veal cutlet, accompanied by a strip of bacon and a fat sausage. Dessert was "Coupe Jamaica," I didn't order it but the couple at the next table did: a long, narrow cookie sticking up out of a ball of vanilla ice cream that rested on a slice of canned pineapple. It would probably confuse Jamaica as much as the chicken would confuse Maryland. But somebody once told me there's a restaurant in Paris that lists on the menu "Pommes à la French Fries."

*Thursday, July 1*
*Stratford*
*Midnight*

I'm writing this in bed, in a luxurious motel room: wall-to-wall carpet, easy chair, TV set, dressing table and a beautiful adjoining bath in mauve tile, life at the Kenilworth was never like this.

I tell you my Colonel has got to be the world's kindest, most considerate man. We left London in the usual gray weather, it gets to you after a while; I told him I was beginning to crave sunshine the way a thirsty man craves water. We drove into the Cotswolds and about mid-morning the weather cleared and the sun came out briefly. The minute it did, he pulled over to the side of the road, got a deck chair out of the trunk and set it up on a stretch of grass for me so I could lie in the sun the little while it lasted. He told me his wife died of cancer "after two years of hell"; he must have been marvelous through it.

We passed Stoke Poges and he told me that's where Gray's country churchyard is. Gray's "Elegy" was my mother's favorite poem, I'd like to have seen the churchyard but we didn't have time for the detour.

As we drove, he told me a long-winded story about a widow he knows who fell in love with a man and was invited to his villa in Italy, and when she got there she found she had no room of her own, the man actually meant her to share his BEDroom, d'ye see, and Well-I-mean-to-say, said the Colonel, she wasn't aTALL that sort, and it was a shock to find the Bounder wanted only One Thing. I wondered why he told me the story since he didn't figure in it—and then it dawned on me that this was his tactful way of assuring me he didn't expect me to share his bedroom in Stratford. It had never occurred to me; he's much too strait-laced and old-school, it would have been out of character.

He told me he retired from publishing to nurse his wife, and after she died he took the job at Heathrow for the fun of it.

"If I see a man and his wife and grown daughters standing together looking a bit out of sorts, I walk up to the man and say: 'Sir, which of these ladies is your wife?' And he beams! And she beams!" And the Colonel roars with laughter.

"If I see a middle-aged couple looking a bit down, you know, I walk up to them and ask: 'Are you folks on your honeymoon?' and you ought to see their faces! They know I'm joshing—some of 'em do—but still, y'know, they can't help being pleased.

"If I see a child crying—some of them get very tired and upset at a big airport, they're hungry, they want to be at home—and when I see one crying I walk up and ask the parents if they know where I can find a nice little girl because mine is grown up. And then I discover the little girl who's crying and I say she's exactly the sort of little girl I've been looking for, and I ask if she'd consider being my little girl." And he ends each story with that booming laugh of pure pleasure.

The Cotswolds are just what I always thought they'd be: stretches of green countryside pocketed with English villages that seem not to have changed since the time of Elizabeth I. We had lunch at a pub near a country church where, said the Colonel, "Hampden started the Revolution."

Didn't have the nerve to tell him I don't know who Hampden was.

Stratford is beyond Oxford, we backtrack tomorrow. We passed Oxford road signs and I told him about Great Tew. Years ago, somebody sent me a postcard—a photograph of five thatched cottages falling down a hillside—and wrote on the back:

> This is Great Tew. You can't find it on the map, you have to get lost on the way to Oxford.

The photo was so idealized a view of rural England I didn't believe the village really existed. I used to stare at that postcard by the hour. Kept it for years, stuck in my Oxford English Verse.

"Well!" said the Colonel, inspired by the challenge. "We shall just have to find Great Tew and see if it's still the same."

He wove in and out through the Cotswolds and finally we came to signs pointing to Tew and Little Tew and rounded a curve and there was Great Tew, looking exactly as it had looked on my postcard: five ancient stone houses with thatched roofs, still falling down the hillside. The Colonel said they date back to Henry VIII. Five hundred years later they're still lived in: there were white curtains and flower boxes at the windows, and every front lawn had a rose garden.

He parked the car—the only car in sight—and we got out. Down the road from the cottages was the village's only other building, a one-room General Store and Post Office.

We went in. There was no one in there but the woman who runs it, and we hadn't seen a soul outside.

The Colonel bought ice cream, I asked for a glass of milk and was handed a quart bottle and a straw. The Colonel told the proprietress that I had come "all the way from New York" and had "particularly asked to see Great Tew." While they talked I was clutching the quart bottle entirely preoccupied with trying to get at least half a pint of it inside me so as not to hurt her feelings. When I'd drunk that much I looked around for an inobtrusive place to park the bottle, and discovered that the store had suddenly filled up with people—men in country caps and women in print dresses. I moved out of their way and they all stepped up to the counter and bought cigarettes and newspapers. A few children came in and were promptly shooed out by the proprietress.

The Colonel finished his ice cream, took my milk bottle off my hands and disposed of a pint and a half of milk as if it were a glass of water, and we left.

"Well!" he said as we walked back to the car. "We've given them something to talk about for a month! Did you notice how the entire village came in to see the people from Outer Space? As soon as they saw my car with the London plates they came running. Did you see how she shooed the kids out? That was to make room for all the grownups. They won't see travelers here from one year's end to the next. And from New York? Not in a lifetime!"

And we were a few hours from London by car.

Everybody I ever knew who went to Stratford had warned me it was a commercial tourist trap, so I was prepared for it. The first thing we saw as we drove in was a huge billboard advertising the JUDITH SHAKESPEARE WIMPY HAMBURGER BAR, the Colonel was purple with fury. It doesn't matter in the least. You find Shakespeare's house and pay your fee to enter—and just to walk up the stairs gripping the huge railing, just to walk into the bedroom and touch the walls, and then come back down and stand in the kitchen that saw him in and out every day of his growing up has to melt the bones of anyone born speaking English.

We saw *Much Ado* at the shiny modern theater, very conventional, not very well acted. The Colonel slept through most of it and I didn't blame him.

Will now go climb into that mauve bathtub, we leave for Oxford early in the morning and I mean to get the most out of this posh palace first.

I saw Trinity College and walked the Yard John Donne walked; I saw Oriel and sat in John Henry's chapel. And what I went through to see them, you purely will not credit. I think I finally had a temper tantrum. I hope I did.

We reached Oxford a little before noon and found the Davidsons' house on a typical tree-shaded, college-town street. Laura was there waiting for us. She said the Professor was working and son David was in school counting the hours till he could join us for tea.

She has a throaty voice and a lovely, odd accent; she was born in Vienna and grew up in England. She and her husband were both refugee children from Hitler's Germany.

She was vastly amused by the Colonel, she called him "the Commahnder" and said he reminded her of Winnie the Pooh. My problem was that by this time the Colonel and I had already had thirty straight hours of Togetherness and I'm not equipped for it, not even with the best friend I have on earth, which he isn't. Over lunch in a campus pub, he announced (*à propos* of nothing, I think he was just carried away by Oxford):

"The British Empire will be brought back by popular demand! An Egyptian said to me recently: 'Why do you English sit modestly at home when you're needed all over the world?'"

For some reason this aggravated me and I said something rude, and we had at it for a couple of minutes till Laura tactfully inserted herself between us like a house-mother, and restored harmony.

After lunch, my troubles started. I said Could we

please go see Trinity and Oriel Colleges? and Laura said First we must visit the Bodleian Reading Room, it was a magnificent Wren building and her husband was working there and wanted to meet me. We went there and I met the Professor and saw the Reading Room, vaulted ceiling, towering shelves and staircases, all spectacular.

We came out, and I said Now could we go see Trinity and Oriel? and Laura said Did I know the Bodleian library stacks ran for a mile under the pavements? and showed me which pavements. And the Colonel said he had studied one summer at Wadham College and I must see Wadham Yard. And he and Laura agreed they must take me down the main street to Blackwell's Bookshop, very famous bookshop and they both knew how interested I was in bookshops. (I despair of ever getting it through anybody's head I am not interested in bookshops, I am interested in what's written in the books. I don't browse in bookshops, I browse in libraries, where you can take a book home and read it, and if you like it you go to a bookshop and buy it.)

So, on the one shining day of my life when I was actually in Oxford, I'm dragged down the main street, I'm having every monument and every church pointed out to me, they're all by Wren (everything's by Wren), I'm hauled through Blackwell's Bookshop table by table and shelf by shelf, and the next thing I know I'm walking around the Yard of some place called Wadham, for God's sake. And it's getting later and later, any minute we'll be off to Laura's house to meet her son for tea and after tea the Colonel and I will be leaving for London.

So I had a tantrum.

I stood in the middle of Wadham Yard and hollered:

"WHEN ARE WE GONNA SEE SOMETHING *I* WANNA SEE?"

Laura hurried over to me and got very kindly and understanding (she used to be a Social Worker) and said:

"The Commahnder's loving it. Wadham is his only link with Oxford."

And I replied reasonably: "HE LIVES OVER HERE, HE CAN SEE IT ANY DAMN DAY HE WANTS TO!"

And she said Sh-sh, and the Colonel strode over and said What is it? What's the matter? And they both thought it over and decided I was right, Now what was it I specially wanted to see? And Laura said Was I sure there was an Oriel College, she couldn't find it on her map, and the Colonel said Was I perhaps thinking of Trinity-Cambridge, Prince Charles had gone to Trinity-Cambridge.

And I said carefully No, I was thinking of John Henry Newman, who taught Anglican theology at Oriel College and died a Catholic cardinal and was a little cracked in many ways but who wrote English like few men on God's green earth ever wrote English, one of the few being John Donne, and they both went to Trinity-OXFORD, so could I please see Trinity and Oriel.

We came out of Wadham Yard and stood on a corner and Laura studied her map again and sure enough, there was an Oriel College. We went there and I sat in the chapel by myself and communed with John Henry. (Outside, I learned later, the Colonel was telling Laura I was "a crazy, mixed-up kid.")

We went to Trinity and I walked around the Yard. And that was all. Tourists are not allowed inside the college buildings.

Unless you're interested chiefly in the architecture,

visiting Oxford is very frustrating. All that is open to tourists at any college is the Yard outside it and the chapel just inside the front door. Everything else is off limits. So I'll never see those freshman's rooms and I'll never know whether there is still "much snap-dragon" growing outside the window, as there was in Newman's day. And I'll never see the rooms Milton wrote in or the rooms Q taught in at Cambridge because Cambridge has the same restrictions.

We got back to Laura's house—five minutes before fifteen-year-old David came home panting and breathless, he'd run all the way just to meet me, I've never been so flattered.

The Colonel had a cup of tea and then marched off to a bedroom and took a nap, and Laura and David and I sat in the kitchen and swapped stories about Philadelphia, where their home is and where I grew up. They go back in September.

Over tea, Laura got very guilt-ridden about my day and begged me to sneak back up on a train one day and do Oxford by myself. ("Don't even let us know you're here if you don't want to," she said, and David said, "Why can't she let us know she's here?") I told her I'd seen what I most wanted to see—and within the limits of what was possible, it was true.

Driving back to London we passed a village called Thame—pronounced as spelled, like "same" with a lisp—and the Colonel told me why the Thames is pronounced Temmes. Seems the first Hanover king had a thick German accent and couldn't pronounce *th*. He called the river "te Temmes" and since the-king-is-always-right everybody else had to call it the Temmes and it's been the Temmes ever since.

He told me about all the widows who depend on him for advice, they all seem to have "lashings of money" and children who adore him.

We got home at nine. I'll be grateful to him all my life for the trip, but it was a lot of togetherness. I holed up in the bar to write this; the Lounge is more comfortable and also free but anybody who talked to me tonight would've got bit.

Flock of messages for me at the desk. Marc Connelly phoned, the London *Reader's Digest* phoned, Nikki's Barbara phoned and a woman I never heard of phoned. The desk clerk was very impressed by all the messages. So was I.

*Saturday, July 3*

I just called Marc Connelly. He was a reigning playwright when I was a child and my parents were rabid theatergoers. They should have lived to see the fan letter he wrote me. It came just before Christmas and I almost threw it away without opening it. His name is on some way-out charity I don't care for, and I thought the letter was another appeal. Not till my hand was hovering over the wastebasket did it occur to me that the envelope was very thin for a charity appeal. So I opened it.

Dear Miss Hanff:

What with all those other letters closing in on you (How many grateful people have written up to now—one million? two million?) I don't expect you'll get around to reading this for a year or more.

Anyway, sooner or later you'll find it's just like all the others: telling you that "84, Charing Cross Road" is tender and funny and incandescent and beautiful and makes the reader rejoice to be living in the same century with you.

Genuflections,

Marc Connelly

And I almost threw it away without opening it.
I met him a few months later, and he told me he'd be

in London in July, at his club, and he'd take me to see what a gentleman's club looks like.

He'll pick me up tomorrow at one for lunch.

Can't call Nikki's Barbara or the *Reader's Digest* till Monday, both offices are closed Saturdays. Nikki—the friend whose deviled egg Chester-the-Sheep-Dog sat on at our Central Park picnic—works for a news magazine in New York. Barbara works for the same news magazine in London. The two girls have never met but they talk to each other every day over the teletype so they're good friends. Nikki made us promise to meet while I'm here.

I can definitely make it till the fifteenth, dinner invitations coming in nicely. I just phoned that woman I never heard of who called while I was away. She said she and her husband are fans of the book and want me to come to dinner to see their part of London. I'm going there Tuesday.

Every breathing tourist who has breakfast in this hotel has seen a piece of royalty but me. (How I know is, whoever is breakfasting alone at the next table strikes up a conversation with you, usually beginning with, "*Might* I trouble you for the marmalade?") Either they saw the Family leave for Windsor, or they were getting on the elevator at Harrods just as the Queen Mother was getting off it, or they saw Princess Anne wave as she entered the hospital, or they just-by-good-chance happened to be passing by this boys' school as seven-year-old Prince Edward was coming out with the other boys. So this morning I'm going down to Buckingham Palace and try my luck.

*10 p.m.*

Went down to Buckingham Palace, walked up and down along the spiked iron fence for a while but all I saw was one more anachronism: a seventeenth-century carriage drawn by white horses, driven through the gates by a fancy-dress coachman, and inside the carriage a pair of cold-eyed diplomats in top hats with cigarettes hanging out of their twentieth-century faces.

I find the treatment of royalty distinctly peculiar. The royal family lives in palaces heavily screened from prying eyes by fences, grounds, gates, guards, all designed to ensure the family absolute privacy. And every newspaper in London carried headlines announcing PRINCESS ANNE HAS OVARIAN CYST REMOVED. I mean you're a young girl reared in heavily guarded seclusion and every beer drinker in every pub knows the precise state of your ovaries.

Walked home by way of Lincoln's Inn Fields, a park this side of the Inns of Court facing a lovely row of houses on a street called King's Bench Walk. Sat on a bench and looked at the houses and listened to the conversations going by:

". . . well, not uncouth, he looks like a Highland rabbi."

". . . but she wasn't getting anywhere out there so she packed it in and now she's home, looking . . ."

"They're all out to save their own neckties, you can bloody bet on that!"

I'm in the bar again. I don't normally drink after dinner but in this hotel they think you're strange if you drink *before* dinner. So at 10 P.M. I'm having a martini. More or less.

The first night I came in here I said to the young bartender:

"A martini, please."

He reached for a bottle of Martini & Rossi vermouth and poured a glass full of it before I could scream WAIT A MINUTE!

"Would you put the gin in first, please?" I asked.

"Oh!" he said. "You want a *gin* martini."

He got the gin bottle and a shaker, and I said:

"Would you put some ice in the shaker, please? I like it cold."

"Right-o!" he said. He put an ice cube in the shaker, poured a jigger of gin on it, added half a cup of vermouth, stirred once, poured it out and handed it to me with a flourish. I paid him and shuffled over to a table telling myself sternly.

"Don't be like all those American tourists who can't adapt to another country's customs, just drink it."

Nobody could drink it.

The next time I came in it was dinner time, the bar was empty and the bartender and I got chummy; he said Wasn't I the writer? and told me his name was Bob. I said Did he mind if this time we used my recipe instead of his and he said Right-o, just tell him exactly what I wanted.

I said First could we start with four ice cubes in the shaker. He thought I was crazy but he put three cubes in (he was short on ice). He poured a jigger of gin in the shaker and I said:

"Okay, now another jigger of gin."

He stared at me, shook his head in disbelief and added a second jigger of gin.

"Okay, now one more," I said.

"MORE gin?" he said, and I said:

"Yes, and lower your voice."

He poured the third jigger, still shaking his head. He reached for the vermouth bottle, and I said:

"I'll pour that."

I added a few drops of vermouth, stirred vigorously, let him pour it out for me and told him it was perfect.

Now he makes it by himself but he never can bring himself to add that third jigger of gin, he thinks he'll look up later and see me sprawled face down on a bar table sodden drunk.

*Sunday, July 4*

Got very gloomy remembering the days before the Viet Nam War when I gloried in my country's history and July 4 meant something.

Marc Connelly picked me up at one. I wore the brown skirt and white blazer, and he said, "Don't you look fine in your little yachting outfit," and saluted. He said we'd have lunch at the Hilton because nothing else is open.

The Hilton has several dining rooms, he took me into the largest. It was crowded with sleek, well-groomed men and beautifully dressed women; nobody looked dowdy the way they do at the Kenilworth. And the strawberries were huge and the cream was thick and the rolls were hot and the butter was cold and the chicken livers were done to perfection.

But at the Kenilworth, nobody sends the eggs back. Nobody talks to the waiters with the casual rudeness that says, "I am better than you are because I am richer." And the waiters don't answer with that studied blend of contempt and servility, and none are obsequious—my God, Alvaro couldn't even pronounce it. And nobody at a Kenilworth breakfast table looks bitter or discontented, no men at the Kenilworth moodily drink their lunch, no women with hard-painted faces keep a sharp eye on their handbags.

You look at the faces in the Hilton dining room and first you want to smack them and then you just feel sorry for them, not a soul in the room looked happy.

After lunch Marc took me to his club on St. James's Street. The building looks narrow from the street; but you step through the doorway into an enormous drawing room with other large rooms beyond it, you climb a great curved staircase, the wall alongside lined with portraits of club presidents all looking like Peter Ustinov, and upstairs you find more spacious rooms—breakfast rooms, game rooms, reading rooms. We watched cricket for a while on color TV in one of the game rooms. At least, I watched it. Marc went to sleep. He's eighty, he's allowed.

I woke him at three to say I was leaving and he said cheerfully, "Now you know what I think of cricket!" and saw me to the door and told me to walk down Jermyn Street and look in the shop windows.

I did that, and then went over to Regent and was walking down Waterloo on my way to St. James's Park when who should I run into, standing on a corner on a little pedestal looking small and spruce, but Gentlemanly Johnny Burgoyne who lost the Battle of Saratoga to us rebels. I think he was supposed to link up with some other general's forces but there was a snafu and Burgoyne's entire army was captured. He'd be pleased to know he's the most appealing character in *The Devil's Disciple*, he was a playwright himself. He wrote a play and produced it in Boston, with his officers in the cast, when his troops occupied the city. Can't imagine what possessed the British to put up a statue to him, I suppose he won some battle somewhere but he lost the American Revolution almost singlehanded.

Wished him a happy Fourth.

When I got down to the Mall there was a band concert going on. In honor of the Fourth of July the band played "Dixie" and "The Battle Hymn of the Republic." Well, why not? I don't know who Hampden was, why should they know July Fourth doesn't commemorate the Civil War?

Sunned myself in St. James's Park for a while but the band concert went on and on and I wasn't in the mood so I thought I'd walk up to Lincoln's Inn Fields instead. I couldn't get back up the broad marble steps, they were jammed with concert listeners, so I walked along the Mall looking for another exit. I came to a small flight of steps, maneuvered my way around the people sitting on them and came up into Carlton Gardens, a beautiful street of very plush apartment houses. It reminded me a little of Sutton Place: the buildings, the expensive cars at the curb, the starched nanny going by pushing a pram, all reeked of money. I walked around it and maybe I walked along an adjoining street, I'm not sure. Then I turned a corner and found myself on a street I had not been on before and the likes of which I never expect to be on again.

I don't even know where I was. I could find no name to the street, I'm not even sure it was a street. It was a kind of enclosed courtyard, a cul-de-sac behind Clarence House and St. James's Palace. The anonymous white buildings on it might be the backs of the palaces. The white stone glows sumptuous and the street is absolutely still. A footstep is loud and you stand without moving, almost without breathing. There is no reek of money here, only the hallowed hush of privilege. Your mind fills with stories of the fairy-tale splendor of monarchy, the regal pomp of England's kings and queens. And then suddenly you remember Karl Marx in an untroubled grave in Highgate, and Queen Mary welcoming Gandhi as she had welcomed the rajahs before him, as George III had been forced to welcome as Ambassador to the Court of St. James old upstart John Adams. You are awed by the contrasts—by the *fact* of St.

James's and Clarence House resting so serenely in Socialist England.

You decide to stop using the word "anachronism" when a seventeenth-century carriage drives through the gates of Buckingham Palace carrying twentieth-century Russian or African diplomats to be welcomed by a queen. "Anachronism" implies something long dead, and nothing is dead here. History, as they say, is alive and well and living in London.

*Monday, July 5*

Nikki's Barbara phoned this morning; we made a lunch date for Friday. I gave her a couple of questions to ask Nikki over the teletype, she'll bring the answers to lunch with her.

I called the *Reader's Digest* office and the girl there said they're using the fan-mail article in the English edition but it deals only with American fan mail, didn't I have any English fans? Shades of the Colonel, didn't I just. I explained that the article was written and sold before the English fan mail arrived, and she said Would I dreadfully mind writing a page or two about the English fan mail? They go to press in a few days, they would have to have the new pages tomorrow, could I possibly?

I felt like saying, "Lady, this is the first real vacation I've ever had in my life and I've only got ten days of it left!" But unfortunately it crossed my mind that I wouldn't be having the first real vacation of my life if it weren't for the *Reader's Digest*, so I said it would be a pleasure.

Will now shlep up the street to Deutsch's and borrow a typewriter.

*Later*

Wrote three new pages and took them down to the *Digest* office in Berkeley Square and walked home by a lovely new route, straight up the Visitors' Map to the Regent's Park area and then over. Somewhere along the way I came upon a mews with a small sign on the entrance gate addressed to the passing world. The sign orders flatly:

## COMMIT NO NUISANCE

The more you stare at that, the more territory it covers. From dirtying the streets to housebreaking to invading Viet Nam, that covers all the territory there is.

There was a letter at the desk for me when I came back:

Can you be here Wednesday at noon *sharp*, for a visit to two stately homes of England?

In haste—

P. B.

Mary Scott just phoned. She wrote me last spring that she and her husband are Californians who spend every spring and summer in London, and she offered to take me on a walking tour. She told me she's had house guests for a month, they've just left and she's finally free for that walking tour, she'll pick me up for the tour Thursday morning and take me home to dinner afterwards.

Tomorrow night I'm having dinner with the English couple who phoned me while I was in Stratford, and the Scotts are feeding me Thursday, so I may just spring for a hairdresser on the dinner money I'm saving.

*Tuesday, July 6*

Had my hair done at a little shop out Regent's Park way on Paddington Street, and the pretty hairdresser asked Was I from the States, and I said Yes.

"How do you find London?" she asked. "Do the noise and the crowds bother you?"

The what?

For a big city, London is incredibly quiet. The traffic is worse than at home because the streets here are so narrow; but the cars are very quiet going by in the street and there are no trucks at all, a city ordinance bans them. Even the sirens are quiet. The ambulance sirens go *BlooOOP, blooOOP,* like a walrus weeping under water.

And I haven't seen anything here, not even on a bus, that a New Yorker would describe as a crowd.

*Midnight*

Those English fans who invited me to dinner are a charming couple, they live in Kensington in a mews. A mews is an alley built originally for stables and carriage barns, and the fad is to convert the barns and stables into modern homes, everybody wants to live in a converted stable, it's chic.

But stables and carriage barns were built of stone and they don't have windows. And the horses weren't interested in indoor plumbing or electricity. You buy one of these stables and kill yourself turning a horse's stall into a very peculiar kitchen (cramped between two high stone partitions); you wire all the stalls for electricity, you pipe them for water, you get all your kitchen and bathroom equipment and furniture moved into the proper horses' stalls—and when you're all through you still can't chop a hole through a foot-thick stone wall for windows, so you have everything you need but air. The couple I had dinner with live in a charming little stable which, they explained to me cheerfully, is so hot all summer they get out of it as soon after supper as possible. In winter they freeze without heat and suffocate with it.

Across the street from them is Agatha Christie, just as comfortably situated and a lot older.

Demented.

They fed me an elegant salmon steak and drove me through Chiswick—pronounced Chizzick—and we walked along the Strand on the Green. The Strand on the Green is a lovely avenue overlooking the Thames, you can run down the front steps of the houses and jump in the river. The houses were built by Charles II for his mistresses. They are very beautiful and charming, very expensive and sought-after, and the elite who live in them are envied just as much as if the Thames didn't overflow every now and then and flood all their living rooms.

I don't remember what we were talking about, but I described something-or-other in Central Park and my hostess looked at me in horror.

"You mean you actually go into Central Park?" she asked. "I thought people got killed there."

I said I was in it almost every day, and offered to take her and her husband on a guided tour of it if they ever came to New York. And then they told me that last year they spent three days at the Plaza Hotel and never left their hotel room for fear of being killed. They didn't walk down Fifth Avenue. They didn't see the park, even from a hansom cab. They didn't set foot in a single skyscraper. They didn't get on a sight-seeing bus.

*They never left their room.*

"We were too terrified," the wife said.

Since I arrived in London, three college boys have been found shot to death as they slept at a camp site; a girl was found stabbed to death in her flat; and there are signs all over town reading LOCK UP LONDON. I asked PB about them, he said they're part of a campaign to get Londoners to lock doors and windows when they go out because of the wave of robberies; three of his friends' flats were robbed in one weekend.

Crime is a hundred times worse in New York. We probably have more murders and muggings there in a week than London will see in a year. Still, for what it's worth, no umpire or fan in Shea Stadium will ever take his eyes off the baseball diamond long enough to make a pass at a girl. And no New York dog will attack three children on the street, killing one of them, which happened here last week.

I mean things are tough all over. Tougher in New York. But not so tough as to justify two Londoners huddling together in a hotel room for a weekend, *declining* the only chance they'll ever have to see the one fabulous city the twentieth century has created.

One of these days I'm going to write a book about living in New York—in a sixteen-story apartment house complete with families, bachelors, career girls, a ninety-year-old Village Idiot and a doorman who can tell you the name and apartment number of every one of the twenty-seven resident dogs. I am so tired of being told what a terrible place New York is to live in by people who don't live there.

PB took me to Syon House, the ancestral home of those miserable Northumberlands who tried to make Jane Grey queen and sided with Mary of Scotland against Elizabeth. The rose gardens there are beyond anything I've seen: acres of roses in a spectacular rainbow of colors. PB told me he spent the weekend with friends in the country who had a double rose garden and didn't offer him so much as a bud to take home. Londoners miss their gardens, he and the other tenants in his building do a little gardening in pots on the roof.

We went from Syon House to Osterly Park, another ancestral home, I forget whose. I'm learning a little about Nash houses and Wren churches; today at Osterly Park it was Adam walls: polished wood panels covered with intricate marquetry. You can examine a single wall for hours and not see all the details in the carving. In a century dominated by watches, cars, planes, schedules, it's hard to imagine an age in which men had the endless time and patience needed for such work.

Driving home, PB told me he worked in Hollywood off and on for years as a consultant on films with English locales. The notion of PB in Hollywood in its heyday, when it was a synonym for everything tasteless and overdone, was grotesque at first, but then I realized he's one of those originals who would be at home in almost any setting; nothing rubs off on him. He's been everywhere and knows everybody, he's very social—there are always a dozen invitations propped up on the mantel—but he seems always a little apart from those around him.

He told me he once spent months hauling an American architect all over England for the Essex House in New York. The Essex House was doing over its cocktail lounge and wanted to re-create an English pub.

"They sent a chap over here to see me and I drove him round the country to see all the best of the old pubs. He went back to New York and drew up the plans and sent them to me. I'll show them to you when we get home."

We got back to Rutland Gate and he showed me the drawings and they were marvelous: a pub with wood-paneled walls, antiqued wooden tables and benches and a high, old-fashioned wooden bar with kegs above it. The pub looked warm and mellow and the woods burnished in the glow of old-fashioned lamps that swung from the ceiling.

"Is the pub still there?" I asked.

"I think so," he said.

"I'll go see it when I get home," I said. "Did he write and tell you how it looks?"

"Oh, yes"—in that light, noncommittal voice—"the Essex House did the pub in lucite, chrome and black leather."

He goes to Wales for a week on Saturday. I'll be gone when he gets back.

Mary Scott took me on a walking tour of Knightsbridge and Kensington, we went to Harrods first because I'd never seen it. It's an incredible store, you can buy anything from a diamond necklace to a live tiger, they have a zoo. I thought of Chester, the sheep dog who lives in my building, he came from Harrods.

On the ground floor there's a florist's shop, and if you want to buy a dozen roses you can choose twelve roses individually. You can pick all buds or all open blooms or half and half, and you can buy one of every color in stock. I ran amok rounding up twelve to send to PB to brighten his flat before he leaves for Wales. Didn't know any other way to thank him.

We wandered the mewses and closes and poked into hidden gardens and alleys. Chelsea, Kensington and Knightsbridge all seem to me self-consciously charming, compared with Regent's Park. The Scotts live out that way and I told Mrs. Scott if I were able to take a flat in London it's out Regent's Park way I'd want to live. She said it's not called Regent's Park, it's called Marylebone.

They have a spacious flat on Gloucester Place and she'd made a beautiful salmon mousse for dinner, loaded with cream. Salmon is a great delicacy here; people serve it as a compliment to their guests the way they serve filet mignon or lobster at home.

Got back here about ten and have had the Lounge to myself for an hour but my luck just ran out. A woman just came in looking for somebody to talk to. She says Be sure and see the Temple, locate Middle Temple Lane and you'll see two large white doors leading into the Temple, the Inner Temple and Middle Temple Hall, and the porter will show you the room where Dickens wrote *Great Expectations*. Doesn't seem the time to tell her I found *Great Expectations* very boring, it's the sort of conversation-stopping sequitur you learn is really *non* sequitur.

She says the Knights Templar were buried under the floor of the church and that's why it's called the Temple. She says the church was destroyed during the war and after the war all the Knights' bones were dug up and they're now in a common grave under the floor of the rebuilt church. It's a good thing I want to see all this, because if I didn't plan to I'd have to keep out of the Lounge, I gather she spends all her evenings in here.

Two women just came in—early thirties, very neat, they may be schoolteachers; they're from Toronto—and it seems the Temple woman sent them somewhere on a day's outing and they are now telling her How Right She Was. Greenwich-by-boat. Maritime Museum.

Temple woman says This will interest me because I'm an American, she says there are Pilgrim artifacts at Greenwich, the Pilgrims took ship from there. Always thought it was Plymouth. Didn't say so. I'm controlling an insane impulse to turn to the three of them and say chattily:

"Did you know that when the Pilgrim Fathers caught a Pilgrim having a love affair with a cow, they not only hanged the Pilgrim, they also hanged the cow?"

One of the teachers wants to know Am I the writer? They've heard such a lot about me at the desk. If they should be able to get a copy of my book tomorrow would I be kind enough to autograph it for them? Soitinly. Told a woman the other night she was passing up a chance to own the only unautographed copy in existence, she just looked at me baffled, nobody understands me.

A man came by at 10 A.M. to interview me for Radio London
and I dragged him and his tape recorder over here, I'm not
sitting in a dark hotel lobby on a sunny summer morning.

He told me a play was done here last season about Lord
Nelson and Lady Hamilton and a script was sent to
Buckingham Palace. It came back to the producer's office
with a note:

> The Duke of Edinburgh thinks you've treated Lady
> Hamilton very shabbily. The Queen reserves judg-
> ment.

Everybody over here has a Philip anecdote for you,
they're proud of the fact that he's so unstuffy. It's appealing
how people regard the Royal Family as relatives, it's a kind
of Cousin-Elizabeth-and-her-husband-and-the-children attitude. So everybody feels free to criticize them, what else
are relatives for? Elizabeth, Philip and Prince Charles all
very popular. Feelings mixed about Princess Anne; most
people I've met are defensive about her. You ask an
Englishman:

"What's Princess Anne like?" and the Englishman
says:

"Well, you must remember she's still very young, she's
new to all this, after all she's only twenty, you can't
expect—"

And all you said was: "What's she like?"

But they're very impressed by her horsemanship, they

tell you with great pride: "She's good enough to ride for England!"

Feelings also mixed (this surprised me) about the Queen Mother. One woman told me:

"Her public image is a masterpiece of press agentry. I once stood next to her at Harrods and caught her eye, and she has the coldest eyes I ever looked into."

Have to go back to the hotel to meet Nikki's Barbara for lunch. She doesn't like curry but she's being magnanimous and taking me to a curry place near me on Charlotte Street.

*Later*

There was a thank-you note at the desk when I got back from Russell Square.

> The super roses arrived—they are on my desk as I write this and perfume the whole room. How very thoughtful—thank you. I just spoke to Jean Ely, she and Ted arrived at the Connaught last night. I thanked her for introducing us.
> Will be back on the 18th. Do be in London still.

In haste—

P.B.

I leave Thursday, the fifteenth.

## VIA TELETYPE

JULY 6, 1971
TO NIKKI FROM HELENE VIA BARBARA    TWO
REQUESTS    FIRST ANDY CAPP COMIC BOOKS
OUT OF PRINT    COULD YOU THINK OF
SOMETHING MORE CULTURED FOR HER TO
BRING YOU    SECOND SHE WOULD LIKE NAMES
OF TWO BEST INDIAN CURRIES SOHO IN THE
NATIVE TONGUE    ALIVE AND WELL

TO BARBARA FROM NIKKI    MANY THANKS FOR
THE MESSAGE FROM HELENE HER POSTCARD
SOUNDS LIKE SHE IS HAVING A BALL    HAVE
YOU MET HER YET

NOT YET BUT AM HAVING LUNCH WITH HER
THIS FRIDAY    DO YOU HAVE CURRIES FOR HER

NOT YET WILL CHECK IT OUT WITH MY
INDIAN FRIEND    AM JUST BACK FROM
VACATION    TELL HER I AM IN LOVE

GOOD FOR YOU    BI

---

JULY 8, 1971
1510 GMT LONDON
TO BARBARA
FROM NIKKI
TWO CURRY NAMES ARE MURGI KARI AND
MURGI MASALAM    ALSO COULD YOU GIVE HER

THE FOLLOWING MESSAGE FROM KEN
MILLS   ALL IS LOST ROOT FOR DODGERS IN
WESTERN DIVISION OR BETTER STILL TAKE UP
CRICKET   HAVE FUN AND THANKS
NIKKI   END

OKAY NIKKI WILL DO   BI

_____

JULY 9, 1971
TO NIKKI NEW YORK
JUST HAD LUNCH WITH HELENE AND
SCRIBBLED OUT THE FOLLOWING MESSAGE FOR
YOU   DUCHESS OF BLOOMSBURY STREET SAYS
HOW THE HELL CAN ALL BE LOST ITS ONLY
JULY   METS WILL START WINNING WHEN SHE
IS HOME TO ROOT THEM THROUGH   DUCHESS
SAYS YOU ARE FORBIDDEN TO ENTER INTO
BETROTHAL WITHOUT HER CONSENT SHE WILL
HAVE TO LOOK HIM OVER FIRST   END

_____

*Saturday, July 10*

I think everybody who works should have Saturday after-
noons off, but they have got goofy ways of managing it over
here.

Went down to Fortnum & Mason to buy small tokens
of esteem for friends back home and by the time I finished
it was lunch time. The store has an attractive coffee shop so
I went there. There was a long line of people waiting for
tables but a few counter seats were empty and I climbed up
on a stool and picked up a menu. People were being served
on both sides of me and the waitress was rushed. I waited till
she'd brought everybody else's tea-and-tart and when she
finally turned to me, I said:

"I'll have a——" and she said:

"We're closed, Madam," and I said:

"You're what?" and she said:

"We're closed."

And she pointed to a waiter who was carrying a
standard to the door. He set the standard down in front of
the long line of people waiting for tables and sure enough,
the sign on the standard said CLOSED.

At high noon on a Saturday with the store open and
jammed with shoppers, the coffee shop closed. Which is
what I call having a good strong Union.

Did the Temple this afternoon. It was raining when I
came out, I took a bus home. You have to watch it with
these buses. A sign on the bus says DO NOT ALIGHT FROM THE
COACH UNTIL REQUESTED TO DO SO. Believe me, it's there for
your health.

The driver is at one end of the bus with his back to the

passengers. Theoretically, the conductor is at the other end, where you get off. But he also has to go through the bus asking new passengers how far they're going and giving them tickets and taking money and making change, and the buses are double decker so half the time he's upstairs.

If he's upstairs when the bus comes to your stop, DO NOT GET OFF THE BUS, just ride past your stop and wait till he comes down. Because if the conductor isn't there to signal the driver when you're safely off, the driver doesn't really stop at your corner, he just slows down there and pauses, and then drives on, on the *assumption* that you're safely off. I'm small and limber, I hopped nimbly off the bus and even so I nearly fell on my face, that bus took off with my left foot on the bottom step.

I just phoned Jean Ely at the Connaught to thank her for asking PB to show me London. She said come to dinner Thursday night, she wants to hear all about it.

*Sunday, July 11*

I saved my three high spots—the Abbey, the Tower and St. Paul's—for the last week and I'm glad I did. Knowing I'm going to see them has kept me from getting depressed about going home when I'm not ready to go home. Woke in high excitement this morning because Sheila and Nora and I were doing the Abbey this afternoon.

It's full of odd things nobody ever told me about—like a plaque to the memory of Major John André, "Mourned Even by His Enemies," it says. "His Enemies" were us rebels. André was the British spy Benedict Arnold betrayed us to. The Americans caught him and hanged him just as the British had caught and hanged Nathan Hale a little earlier. But you wouldn't believe how many American historians make a much bigger fuss over André's death than they do over Nathan Hale's. Nathan Hale was a poor farm boy. John André was a dashing British aristocrat—see. In class-conscious Philadelphia, where André was stationed, you'd better believe he was "Mourned by His Enemies."

It positively outraged me to find Henry Irving buried in Westminster Abbey when Ellen Terry isn't. Henry Irving was one of those legendary actors like Garrick, he was the idol of London in the 1890's. Ellen Terry was his leading lady. I got very fond of her through her correspondence with Shaw and I consider it pure male chauvinism to bury Irving in the Abbey while Ellen's ashes, according to Sheila, are in the little Actors' Church near Covent Garden Market, I'm going there.

Sign of the times: there's a long bench now placed over

one grave so all you can see of the inscription is "Rudyard Ki———."

We passed the War Office when we came out. It was hot today—eighty-four degrees, very hot for London. Outside the War Office, sitting on a horse in the hot sun, was a guard. He wore a solid brass helmet-and-noseplate, which must have been blazing hot. He was dressed in a heavy wool uniform, long leather gloves and leather knee boots, he had a Persian lamb saddle rug tucked around him and he was clutching a spear which was bending slightly from the heat. Bundled up for the Russian Front, all by himself on a hot Sunday, he was guarding the atomic secrets of the War Office with a bent spear. Him and his fur-covered horse.

Sheila says he's there to please tourists like me, he's the fancy-dress London we come looking for. Maybe so. But far away in Wales I could hear a light voice remarking:

"They haven't missed a night in seven hundred years."

On the way back to Highgate for dinner we stopped off at Waterlow Park; it's so high above the city the legend on the park sundial informs you:

THIS SUNDIAL IS LEVEL WITH THE
DOME OF ST. PAUL'S CATHEDRAL

and when you look across the hills the dome is level with your eyes.

In the center of the park there's a two-story house with a high balcony, Sheila told me Charles II built it for Nelly Gwyn. Nell bore him a son there and she kept asking Charles to give the baby a title and Charles kept putting it off. So one day, when she saw the King riding toward the house to visit her, Nelly walked out onto the balcony with the baby in her arms and called down to him:

"If you don't give your son a proper title this instant I shall drop him to his death!"

And Charles II cried:

"Madam, don't drop the Duke of—!" and that's how the baby got his title.

*Later*

Ena just phoned, they're back. They want me to have dinner with them tomorrow night and then see their flat in Ealing. She and Leo will pick me up here at hoppusseven. Nobody over here says "six-thirty" or "seven-thirty," they say "hop-pussix" and "hoppusseven." And "in" at home is "trendy" here and "give it up" is "pack it in" and "never mind!" is "not to worry!"

And when they pronounce it the same they spell it differently. A curb's a kerb, a check's a cheque, a racket's a racquet—and just to confuse you further, "jail is spelled "gaol" and pronounced "jail."

And a newsstand's a kiosk, a subway's the tube, a cigar store's a tobacconist's, a drug store's a chemist's, a bus is a coach, a truck is a lorry, buying on time is hire purchase, cash and carry is cash and wrap and as Shaw once observed, we are two countries divided by a common language. I am now going to bed because it's quataposstwelve.

*Monday, July 12*

O Frabjous Day!

From now on I remember the *Reader's Digest* in all my prayers. I picked up mail at the desk, there was a letter from the London *Digest* office, I assumed it was page proof on the three new pages. I opened it and inside was a check for FIFTY POUNDS, I thought I would die where I stood.

I hunted up Mr. Otto and asked if I could keep the room an extra ten days, he was shocked at the question, he said, "Did you think we'd put you out?!" and clucked.

I tore up the street to Deutsch's to tell everybody the news and Carmen said Ann Edwards of the *Sunday Express* wants to interview me Wednesday over lunch.

"And guess where? The River Room of the Savoy! It's the most divine place in London, I'm so happy for you."

Mr. Tammer couldn't cash the check for me, he said it's made out in such a way only a bank can cash it. Will take it to the bank tomorrow.

I phoned Nora and told her the news and she wants to give a buffet supper for me on Friday to meet all the rare-book dealers, she wanted to do it before but they were all "on holiday."

Joyce Grenfell phoned about dinner tomorrow night, she's putting a note in the mail with complete instructions for finding their flat by bus. It impresses me that in London you can mail an in-city letter on Monday and know for certain it will arrive on Tuesday. In New York you can mail a letter on Monday to an address a block away—and maybe it'll get there on Wednesday and very possibly it won't get there till Thursday.

My social life being what it is, I just faced the fact that I can't get along for two more weeks on one dress. God bless my Democratic Club and my brother, am off to Harrods with the gift certificate and the last of the cash reserve, Ena says they're having a close-out sale of summer dresses.

*Later*

Harrods sale overpriced and mostly midi-skirts they got stuck with. I went up the street to Harvey Nichols and bought a toast-and-white linen on sale and then went back to Harrods and swapped the gift certificate for a sand-colored shoulder bag on sale. Transferred everything to it and threw my old white straw in a Harrods' wastebasket, it's been unraveling for a week.

Took a cab to Johnson's house and lunched at the Cheshire Cheese (money means nothing to me) and stopped at the *Evening Standard* to see Valerie—the girl who interviewed me the day I landed—to tell her the *Standard's* interviewing me over again. (Now-that-I've-been-here-how-do-I-like-it.) While I was there, the catch on my new shoulder bag broke. Valerie was very shocked; I said, "That's why it was on sale." She said, "Yes, but not *Harrods*!" Nobody ever says "Bonwit's" in that tone.

She sent me to a little shop off Fleet Street to have it fixed, and while the man repaired it for me I asked if he could point me toward Bloomsbury, I wanted to walk home. He said:

"Go on up to O-Burn Street and follow the bus."

Looked for O-Burn Street, looked for Auburn Street

and finally stumbled on the street he meant: High Holborn. And that's what they mean by a cockney accent.

Time to go crouch under that sadistic shower and then climb into the new dress for Leo and Ena.

*Midnight*

Leo took us to dinner at a plush seafood restaurant. The shellfish looks the same here as at home but tastes very different; the crabmeat and lobster are much richer here but very bland, almost tasteless to an American palate till you get used to it.

They drove me to their flat and I saw Ena's portrait of Hayley Mills and Pamela Brown. Pamela Brown I have a special love for, dating back to an old, old English film called *I Know Where I'm Going* and to a stage performance I saw her give in *The Importance of Being Earnest*.

I know nothing about painting, not even the right thing to say when you like it; but those faces spoke to you. I was bowled over, I told Ena it's indecent to be that talented when you're pretty and blond and look fresh out of school.

Leo announced he was going to make me his special summer drink, for which he is famous, and he trotted off to the kitchen and banged around and came back with three long, tall drinks. I don't drink after dinner and I don't like carbonated drinks so I don't know one long-tall-drink from another. I sipped this one and said:

"It's ginger ale, isn't it? It's very nice."

"It's gin and tonic," said Leo, wounded.

"The gin kind of gets lost, doesn't it?" I said, and he

loped back to the kitchen for the gin bottle. Ena was doubled up with unkind wifely laughter.

"That's his special drink, he's so proud of it!" she gasped and went off into convulsions. I felt terrible. I told Leo I go through life saying the wrong thing. He put some more gin in my drink and then sat and watched me as I sipped it. When he thought I had enough of it inside me, he said:

"The little thing wants to ask you a favor."

I looked at Ena and said, "What's the favor?" but she just smiled nervously. And Leo said:

"She wants to paint you."

And I said:

"You're crazy."

I know that painters see planes and angles in faces that look commonplace to the rest of us—and I still cannot understand why anyone should want to paint a plain, ordinary middle-aged face. Which I told Ena. To her, I have an interesting face, "it changes all the time." I said I wished it would.

I never felt so trapped. All my life I've avoided being photographed—and here was Ena asking earnestly Would I sit for her? She'd only need a few sittings, "p'raps three or four?" Anxious little face peering at me wistfully.

I told her I'd do it on two conditions: one, she has to paint me in Russell Square, I'm not sitting indoors in some studio; and two, she has to promise not to make me look at the portrait either in progress or when it's finished.

She agreed to both conditions. She's finishing something this week, we start next week.

Paranoid morning.

Joyce Grenfell's note arrived with instructions for finding her flat tonight but nothing on how to find St. Mary LeBeau's Church in Cheapside for her dialogue with the minister at noon. I located Cheapside on my map and then decided to get the *Digest* check cashed before I went down there.

I went to the nearest bank and then to another one across the street from it. Both banks were shocked to be asked to cash a *Reader's Digest* check for a total stranger whose identification they declined to look at. Neither would phone the *Digest* or Deutsch's for me, it wasn't bank policy.

I went to a third bank, where a teller passed me on to an officer who conferred with another officer and then came back and said Wouldn't it be better if I just mailed the check to my bank in New York? I explained that I needed the cash here, which shocked him deeply. You do not say "I need cash" to a banker.

I told him my New York bank was Chemical and asked whether there was a branch in London. He said Yes, reluctantly, but he doubted whether the London bank would cash the check. (He said "could.") I went down to Chemical—and after asking to see everything but my teeth, they cashed it. Nothing infuriates me like those friendly, folksy bank ads in magazines and on TV. Every bank I ever walked into was about as folksy as a cobra.

By this time I had barely half an hour to get down to Cheapside. I got on a bus and discovered I'd forgotten my map. I told the conductor I wanted to go to St. Mary LeBeau's, Cheapside, and he let me off down near St. Paul's, pointed to a yonder street and said:

"Walk that way a bit and turn left."

I walked that way a bit and turned left and walked this way a bit and turned left and turned right and asked six people, all of whom turned out to be tourists. A bus slowed down at a corner, I called to the conductor Could he tell me how to get to St. Mary LeBeau's Church and he called back:

"Sorry, luv, it's m'first day on the job!"

I wished him luck, you might as well, and kept on walking. Found three wrong churches, a Godsmith's Hall and a lot of interesting alleys but no St. Mary LeBeau's. By this time the dialogue was over anyway and I holed up in a smoky little pub and ate myself pleasant.

*Midnight*

Joyce met me at the door and took me on a guided tour of the living-room walls, hung with Grenfell and Langhorne family portraits and photographs. Her mother was one of the Langhorne sisters of Virginia. One sister married Charles Dana Gibson and was the original Gibson Girl, another married Lord Astor and was the famous Lady Astor, M.P., and the third married Joyce's father.

Very few theatrical photos on the wall. The one she's proudest of is the Haymarket marquee with her name in lights. The Haymarket had a rule against putting a star's name in lights, it only lights the name of the show. But when Joyce did her one-man show there, she wasn't just the star, she was the show.

She gave me a biography of Florence Nightingale she thinks I'll like. She sets her alarm for six every morning and reads in bed till seven; she said if she hadn't formed that habit, she'd never find time to read anything. As it is, it seems to me she's read everything.

I'm always so ashamed when I discover how well-read other people are and how ignorant I am in comparison. If you saw the long list of famous books and authors I've never read you wouldn't believe it. My problem is that while other people are reading fifty books I'm reading one book fifty times. I only stop when at the bottom of page 20, say, I realize I can recite pages 21 and 22 from memory. Then I put the book away for a few years.

After dinner they drove me around Chelsea and showed me the house where they were married. Joyce told me they were almost childhood sweethearts.

"I was seventeen and Reggie was just down from Oxford. The first time I played tennis with him I still wore my hair in a braid, I only put it up in the evening."

They drove down into the old City of London and showed me St. Mary–Le–BOW's Church, it now turns out you spell it. Only the English could tack "bow" onto "le." Too dark for me to see where I went wrong.

They kept up an amiable running argument about what to show me.

"Oh, not St. Paul's, dear, she'll have seen that."

"She might like to see it illuminated, RegGEE!"

"She's probably seen it illuminated half a dozen times, why don't you show her Fleet Street?"

I piped up from the back seat that I'd like to see London's slums.

"I'm afraid," said Joyce gently, "there aren't any."

Add that fact to Britain's free medical care and you know all you need to know about the difference between Capitalism and Socialism.

Ann Edwards of the *Sunday Express* took me to lunch at the Savoy and refused to believe I wasn't disappointed in London.

"When I heard you were coming," she said, "I wanted to write you and say, 'My dear, don't come. You're fifteen years too late.'"

For what, Westminster Abbey?

I tried to tell her that if you've dreamed of seeing the Abbey and St. Paul's and the Tower all your life, and one day you find yourself actually there, they can't disappoint you. I told her I was finally going to St. Paul's when I left her and I could guarantee her it wouldn't disappoint me. But she's lived in London all her life, she harks back wistfully to the days when her family owned an upright Rolls-Royce, "which, every time it started, coughed gently, like a discreet footman."

The Savoy River Room is beautiful and the food marvelous. (I liked Claridge's better but I romanticize Claridge's.) Had crabmeat and lobster thermidor both, couldn't eat my way through either, the portions were enormous. I finished up with strawberries and cream all the same. English cream is addictive—and every time I eat strawberries here I think of the English clergyman who remarked:

"Doubtless God could have made a better berry than the strawberry and doubtless God never did."

She walked down along the Embankment with me after lunch and pointed me the straightest route to St. Paul's.

It was lovely to walk along the river with John Donne's cathedral looming ahead. Thought about him as I walked, he's the only man I ever heard of who actually *was* a rake reformed by the love of a good woman. He eloped with the daughter of the Lord Lieutenant of the Tower and her outraged papa had them thrown into the Tower for it. John was in one wing, his bride was in another, and he sent her a note, which is how I know he pronounced his name Dunn, not Donn. The note read:

> John Donne
> Anne Donne
> Undone.

He was also a little batty. When Anne died, he had a stone shroud made for himself, and he slept with that shroud in bed with him for twenty years. If you write like an angel, you're allowed to be a bit cracked.

I walked up the steps of St. Paul's—finally, finally, after how many years?—and in through the doorway, and stood there looking up at the domed ceiling and down the broad aisles to the altar, and tried to imagine how Donne felt the night King James sent for him. And for at least that moment, I wouldn't have traded the hundreds of books I've never read for the handful I know almost by heart. I haven't opened Watson's *Lives* in ten years, at least; and standing there in John Donne's cathedral the whole lovely passage was right there in my head:

> When his Majesty was sat down he said after his
> pleasant manner, "Dr. Donne, I have invited you to

dinner and though you sit not down with me, yet will
I carve to you a dish I know you love well. For knowing
you love London I do hereby make you Dean of St.
Paul's and when I have dined, then do you take your
beloved dish home with you to your study, say grace
there to yourself and much good may it do you."

And as Eliza Dolittle would say, I bet I got it right.

There were guides with large tourist parties in tow,
each guide giving the standard lecture, some in English, one
in French, one in German, the monotone voices jarring
against each other. I got as far from them as I could and
wandered around by myself. I went down a side aisle
looking at all the plaques and busts, walked around the altar
and started back up the other side looking at more plaques
and busts. Even so, I almost missed it. It was an odd shape,
it wasn't a bust and it wasn't a full-length statue, so I
stopped and read the inscription. There in front of me,
hanging on the wall of St. Paul's Cathedral, was John
Donne's shroud.

I touched it.

There's a small chapel just inside the door, with a sign
that says: "St. Dunstan's Chapel. Reserved for Private
Meditation." I went in and gave thanks.

Fifteen years too late indeed.

*Thursday, July 15*

Ken Ellis of the London *Reader's Digest* came around this
morning with his pretty assistant and a photographer, to
take my picture. I put up the usual squawk but my heart
wasn't in it (I'd be flying over the Atlantic this minute if it
weren't for the *Digest*) and I trotted meekly back to 84
Charing Cross Road with them and had my picture taken
sitting on the window sill of the bleak, empty upstairs
room. Ken scooped up all the peeled and rusting white
letters that once spelled Marks & Co. for me. I want to take
them home.

(And one September day when I'm doing my fall
cleaning I'll come on them and ask myself, "What do you
want these for—so you can weep over them when you're an
old lady?" and throw them out.)

They took me to Wheeler's for lunch (the famous
seafood restaurant everybody takes you to) and Ken explained to me why everybody over here hates the new
money. It has to do with the Englishman's need to be
different. The decimal system is much simpler than the old
ha'penny-tupenny-guinea-tenner-tanner system, but the old
money was *theirs*; no other country had it and nobody else
could understand it. He said they hate entering the Common Market for the same reason. They don't want to be
part-of-Europe, they want to be separate, different, set apart.
He illustrated this by quoting an old headline which has
become a cliché joke over here. During a spell of bad
weather when the whole island was enveloped in fog, one
English newspaper headline read: FOG ISOLATES CON-
TINENT.

I'm having dinner with the Elys and Jean just called to warn me that the Connaught is very old-world and still doesn't admit women in pants to the dining room, told her with dignity I have two dresses.

*11 p.m.*

The Connaught is near Grosvenor Square so I went there first to see the Roosevelt Memorial. Somebody told me that after Roosevelt's death the British government decided to raise money for the Memorial by public subscription and to limit individual contributions to one shilling so that everyone could subscribe. They announced that the subscription would be kept open as long as necessary to raise all the money in one-shilling contributions.

The subscription closed in seventy-two hours.

The story moved me a lot more than the Memorial did. It's a statue of FDR standing tall, holding a cane, cape flying. The features are there; the character and personality are entirely absent. And I resent a statue of FDR standing on legs that were shriveled and useless throughout his White House life. You can't take the measure of Roosevelt if you ignore the fact that his immense achievements were those of a man paralyzed from the waist down. I'd carve him sitting, with the blanket he always spread over his knees to hide the withered legs. Anything else belittles the gallantry and humor in that indomitable face. Since the gallantry and humor are missing from the statue's face I don't suppose it matters. It's nice to know so many Englishmen loved him, anyway.

Jean and Ted Ely still astonish me. They invited me to dinner in New York after they read the book. They live in a very spacious Fifth Avenue apartment, all polished mahogany and old carpets and warm colors, and I thought they were the most beautiful couple I'd ever seen. Both of them are slim and straight, both have thick gray hair, regular features and serenely smooth faces—and when Jean told me casually they were in their mid-seventies I was stupefied. They are as improbably handsome and untouched by time as the parents of the debutante in a 1930's movie.

We talked about PB through dinner. I sent him a note to tell him I'll be here another two weeks, Jean said maybe he'll take the three of us somewhere.

A chauffeured limousine drove me back here; I do not know how anybody expects me to adjust to life on Second Avenue when I get home.

Ena phoned, How's Sunday morning, am I free to Sit? The things I agree to with a little gin in me.

*Friday, July 16*

Just got back from Nora's buffet supper—where I arrived an hour and a half late and I was the guest of honor, I mean this evening got off to a horrendous start.

Nora had phoned this morning to say a car would pick me up here at seven-fifteen, so as usual I was dressed and waiting in the lobby at seven. No car came at seven-fifteen, no car came at seven-thirty, and by seven-forty-five I decided Nora's friends must have forgotten to pick me up and I called her. She said she'd ordered a cab for me "to bring you out in style." It never came. She told me to go out in the street and hail a cab and come on out.

I went out in the street and hailed a cab and got in. But North London is apparently equivalent to the far end of Brooklyn, and London cab drivers are grimly equivalent to New York cab drivers. I gave the driver Nora's address, and he stared at me mask-like.

"I don't know where that is, Madam," he said in a flat voice. I innocently explained it was in Highgate. He stared straight in front of him this time and repeated in the same expressionless voice:

"I don't know where that is, Madam."

I got the message and got out of the cab and waited ten minutes for the next cab to come along and got in. I gave the driver Nora's address, and we went through the same charade. But this driver was so anxious to get rid of me that when I got out of the cab he shot off before I'd gotten both feet on the ground, and I fell and split my leg open. So there I was, blood all over my leg at eight-fifteen of a seven-thirty supper in my honor. I couldn't go back up to the room and clean the wound and put on fresh stockings because that would have made me fifteen minutes later still.

I went back into the lobby and consulted the desk clerk and he said what I needed was a minicab, they take you anywhere. Minicabs are the London equivalent of New York's limousine services (and cost as much). The clerk phoned the minicab service for me and a cab arrived ten minutes later. The driver told me his name was Barry, he's a hospital intern, he drives a minicab nights to earn a little money. He took the hills of North London like he had a death wish for both of us, but never mind, he got us there and gave me a high old time on the way.

He told me he studied at McGill in Canada and spent summers working in Manhattan. The first day he landed in New York he found himself on the traffic island at Broadway and Forty-second Street, he didn't know where he was, he just knew he wanted to go to Times Square. There was a cop directing traffic, and Barry, wanting to ask directions, stepped up behind the cop and tapped him on the shoulder. Whereupon the cop, true to the tradition of courtesy and helpfulness of New York's Finest, turned around and stuck the muzzle of a gun in Barry's stomach.

"I only want to ask directions to Times Square, Officer," said Barry.

"Izzat right," said the cop.

"I'm a tourist, I don't know my way about," Barry explained. "I'm British."

"No kiddin'," said the cop without taking his gun out of Barry's stomach. So Barry gave up and said:

"Officer, if you're going to shoot me, please step back so you don't kill the four hundred people behind me."

The cop let him go then, and Barry crossed the street and asked a passer-by how to get to Times Square. The passer-by studied the problem thoughtfully and then said:

"Walk one block, turn left, walk one block, turn left, walk one block, turn left and you'll be there."

So Barry walked around the block and that's how he discovered he'd been standing on Times Square all the time. He'd been looking for an English Square—with a park in it. What the passer-by didn't know was that in London you can walk one block, turn left, walk one block, turn left, walk one block, turn left—and be nowhere near where you started from.

He sold Britannicas and fountain pens door-to-door. Most of the housewives slammed the door in his face. ("I used to have to call, 'Madam, will you please open the door so I can get my tie back?'") so he switched to demonstrating fountain pens at Woolworth's. He discovered the way to beat that system was to get very good at it and be promoted to teacher. "Teaching other guys how to demonstrate," he explained, "you at least got to sit down."

He dropped me at Nora's and said he'd pick me up at midnight for the return trip.

I could have brained Nora, she hadn't told the guests I'd been ready-and-waiting since seven-fifteen. One woman turned to me and said politely:

"Do you mind my asking what held you up?" and I was so stunned I couldn't answer her, I just fled upstairs with Sheila and hid out in her room till I got calmed down. I have no poise.

All the rare-book dealers regaled me with stories of the trade. They told me that after the war there were too many books and not enough bookshop space, so all the dealers in London BURIED hundreds of old books in the open bomb craters of London streets. Today the buried books would be worth a fortune if they could be recovered, if the new buildings could be torn down and the rebuilt streets torn up. I had a sudden vision of an atomic war destroying everything in the world, except here and there an old book lying where it fell when it was blasted up out of the depths of London.

Everybody brought me small gifts and I think I made a faux pas with one of them. A very charming woman who deals in autographs gave me a beautifully bound pocket notebook. I needed one, since I'd converted my old one into a calendar, and when the rare-book man from Quaritch's gave me his name and the address of the shop, I wrote them down in the new notebook. From the quality of the silence that followed, I think writing in that notebook was a kind of desecration. I had a horrible feeling the notebook was one of those antique items you're not supposed to use, you're just supposed to look at it. What the hell do I want with a notebook you can't use? I get in trouble this way all the time.

Barry arrived on the dot of twelve and drove me home. He told me to visit his hospital if I get down that way, it's St. Bartholomew's, he said Go in by the Henry VIII gate and see the chapel, it's beautiful. I wrote his name—Barry Goldhill—in the desecrated notebook and asked him what he's specializing in. He said, "Gynecology." I said, "Too late, honey, I can't do a thing for you."

*Saturday, July 17*

Note in the mail from Rutland Gate, he's back.

See you here, Monday, 19th, at 11 *promptly* for sherry
with Charles II and lunch with Charles Dickens.

In haste—

P.B.

I thought I'd better bone up on Dickens first, so after
breakfast I walked out to the Dickens House in Doughty
Street. It's only a few blocks beyond Russell Square, I just
never had enough interest in Dickens to go there before—
which you don't tell to ANYbody over here, it is flat heresy
not to like Dickens. I mean Dickens is the national
household god.

Except for PB, not one single Londoner has ever
mentioned Shakespeare's pub to me. Nobody mentions the
Pepys landmarks, nobody mentions Wimpole Street—and
nobody knows what you're talking about when you ask
about the house where Shaw courted his "green-eyed
millionairess." But every living soul tells you where Mr.
Pickwick dined and where the Old Curiosity Shop is and Do
see the house on Doughty Street where *Oliver Twist* was
written and This is Camden Town, where Bob Cratchit lived
and The-porter-will-show-you-where-Dickens-wrote-*Great-
Expectations*.

Doughty Street is another of those streets lined with
the gentle, narrow brick houses that still shake me. The

Dickens House is furnished much as it was when he lived in it, and the room at the back of the house where he worked has a complete set of Dickens first editions. Walls of every room are crammed with cases of Dickens memorabilia—letters, drawings, cartoons, theatre programs with his name in the cast list. (Never knew he was such a rabid amateur actor.) All the tourists going through the house, mostly from "the U.K.," knew every character and every incident depicted in every drawing and cartoon. Just incredible.

I had lunch at Tanjar's, the curry place on Charlotte Street, and then walked down to Covent Garden to see Ellen Terry's ashes. The church is called St. Paul's Covent Garden but when you get to the Market there's no church in sight. Wandered around, peering at my map and then at Covent Garden Market. A young man with a brown beard came breezing along, went past me, wheeled, came back and inquired:

"Lost, luv?"

I told him I was looking for the Actors' Church and he said: "Are you an actress?"

I said No, but I'd been a frustrated playwright in my youth and I loved the Shaw-Terry correspondence and wanted to see Ellen's ashes.

"Isn't that dear of you," he said. "Nobody ever comes looking for our church but people in the profession."

He's an actor. Out of work. He said Just keep going round the Market till you come to an alleyway, cross it and turn the corner and you'll see the church.

I thanked him and wished him luck and he said, "Luck to you, too, luv!" and went breezing on his way—and looking after him I purely hated myself because I hadn't bothered to ask his name. People oughtn't to breeze into your life and out again in ten seconds, without leaving even a name behind. As Mr. Dickens once pointed out, we're all on our way to the grave together.

I picked my way through the rotting fruits and vegetables lying on the pavement in front of the Market, walked to the corner and came to the alley, a kind of open square used for parking produce trucks and littered with garbage. I crossed the alley and turned the corner and there it was—a small church in a green churchyard, with a garden beyond.

The church was empty. For which I was grateful. I am emotional, and if you're emotional you never know what may suddenly move you to tears. I thought Ellen's ashes might.

There was a pile of mimeographed sheets on a table, and a sign invites the visitor to take one and sit down and read it so you'll know "something about where you are." The church was built by Inigo Jones back in the 1630's. William S. Gilbert was baptized there, Wycherley is buried there, Davy Garrick worshipped there—and Professor Enry Iggins first saw Eliza Dolittle selling her flaaars under the church portico in the rain.

I went along the right-hand wall reading plaques to the memory of long-dead actors and composers. Almost at the end of the wall, near the altar, in a niche behind iron grillwork in a silver urn polished to a pristine gleam, Ellen Terry's ashes. Surprised to find myself smiling at the urn; it's a luminous, cheerful sight.

I crossed the nave and came back up along the left-hand wall and read more plaques clear to the door. Just inside the door as I was leaving I came upon the most recent plaque:

VIVIEN LEIGH D. 1967

and was suddenly moved to tears.

Sat.

Ena picked me up in a clattery station wagon and drove me to Russell Square and parked at the entrance. The station wagon has sliding doors which I naturally tried to open outward, nearly broke the door and my arm both. Ena was convulsed, and said: "You're exactly like Leo!" It seems he never gets the hang of anything mechanical either.

I got out and she climbed out after me, all five feet of her, lugging a six-foot easel, a four-foot box of paints, a palette, some magazines and a radio the size of a portable TV set. I wasn't allowed to help: the Subject is not permitted to fetch-and-carry.

We set up deck chairs—lounge chair for me, straight-backed one for her—and I was surprised and relieved to learn that when you Sit you don't have to sit still and hold a pose. Ena told me I could lie back, sit up, stretch, move, smoke, anything as long as I kept facing her. She then went into great detail about how to operate the radio; it turned out she'd brought the radio and magazine for me, to keep me from getting bored. It struck me funny.

"I don't get bored in Russell Square and I don't get bored with you," I told her. "Can't we talk while you work?"

"Oh, I'd love that," she said. "None of my subjects ever talks to me. They sit in silence hour after hour."

"With me," I said, "that is not likely to be your problem."

My friend the ticket taker came over to stand behind her and watch her paint. So did two English ladies, an

Indian student and a middle-aged Jamaican with a walking stick.

"How's she doing?" I asked them, only wanting to be sociable. But being spoken to directly seemed to embarrass them and they mumbled, "Very good," and, "Very nice," and melted away. Ena thanked me, she said the gallery made her nervous. So from now on my function is to shoo away what New Yorkers call the Sidewalk Superintendents. In London you shoo them away by talking to them. In New York talking to them would just get you their life stories.

It's fascinating to watch a portrait painter work. There Ena sat, her red-and-white gingham dress flouncing around her, looking completely relaxed, talking, laughing, asking questions as she painted—and all the time, her eyes were darting with incredible speed up to my face, down to the easel, up to the face, down to the easel, up-down up-down up-down, in a motion as quick and sharp and rhythmic as a metronome at high speed. Hour after hour she talked and laughed and painted, and the quick up-and-down darting of the eyes never stopped for an instant. I tried it myself for about twenty seconds and my eye muscles were sore.

She painted till one and then drove me down to Kensington for lunch. We didn't try to talk on the way; the station-wagon clatter was as deafening as a New York subway. English cars are blissfully quiet going by you in the street but very noisy to ride in. American cars exactly the opposite.

She took me to a little Italian place for lunch, down near where she and Leo live, called Panzer's Pasta and Pizza, it's their favorite neighborhood hangout. I had the best martini I've had in London and a chicken-with-garlic-butter they can serve me in heaven.

Ena was shocked that I hadn't been to a single gallery and firmly dragged me to the National Portrait Gallery after lunch—where I amazed myself by going clean out of my mind meeting old friends face-to-face. Charles II looks exactly the dirty-old-man he was, Mary of Scotland looks exactly the witch-on-a-broomstick she was, Elizabeth looks marvelous, the painter caught everything—the bright, sharp eyes and strong nose, the translucent skin and delicate hands, the glittering, cold isolation. Wish I knew why portraits of Mary and Elizabeth always look real and alive, and portraits of Shakespeare, painted in the same era and the same fashion, always look stylized and remote.

I stared at every face so long we never got out of the sixteenth and seventeenth centuries. We're going back next week for the eighteenth and nineteenth, I am now passionately determined to see everybody.

The Colonel phoned, he's driving me into the country for dinner on Wednesday.

Got to Rutland Gate at eleven. That's a lie. I'm always so afraid I won't get there *"promptly"* I always take a cab, I always get there twenty minutes early and walk around the neighborhood till it's late enough to ring his bell. I enjoy it, it's an interesting neighborhood.

He took me to the Old Wine Shades in Martin Lane, Cannon Street, for sherry-at-eleven. It's the only pub in London that survived the Great Fire of 1666. It was built before 1663 and doesn't seem to have changed since. There are ancient wine kegs over the bar, the wooden tables and benches are age-stained, even the menu sounded archaic, I could imagine Sam Pepys ordering the Veal and Sweetmeat Pie.

He took me to the Bank of England, where the doormen and floorwalkers are dressed in red waistcoats and breeches, and bow as they bid you good morning. (Aside from them, it's just one more folksy cobra.)

We had lunch at the George & Vulture where, it quotes on the menu, "Mr. Pickwick invited about five-and-forty people to dine with him the very first time they came to London." The restaurant is the headquarters of the Pickwick Club. Dickens cartoons on the walls; steaks and chops done over an open fire in a great stone fireplace.

Around the corner from the George & Vulture is "the Church of St. Michael Cornhill with St. Peter Le Poer and St. Benet Fink." I'm putting St. Benet Fink on my Favorite Saints list right under the two New Orleans saints.

Back around 1801, when the U.S. bought Louisiana, American firms moved in on the Catholic icon business and began sending crates of church statuary down to New Orleans. The crates were labeled FRAGILE and EXPEDITE. New Orleaners were French, they couldn't read English and they didn't know what the two words meant. They decided the words must be the names of two new saints whose icons were inside the crates. Next thing anybody knew, the most popular saints in New Orleans were St. Fragile and St. Expedite.

St. Fragile lost ground after a while but the last I heard you could still pick up a New Orleans newspaper any day and read in the Personals Column:

> Thanks to St. Expedite for
> special favor granted.

According to the icons, he's an ancient Roman, he wears a toga. Wish I knew as much about St. Benet Fink, PB didn't know who he was.

We walked Lombard Street, PB said the London banking business was founded by Jews from Lombardy in the 1400's. Each money lender hung out an emblem to identity his establishment, and from then on Lombard Street banks all hung out emblems on brass plates. The emblems still swing in the breeze: the Bank of Scotland's emblem is a Cat-and-a-Fiddle, another bank has a Grasshopper, a third has a Rampant Horse. PB didn't know where the symbols came from or what they originally meant, they're hundreds of years old. (So along comes the U.S. and opens a bank on Lombard Street and sees all these cats-and-fiddles and grasshoppers and rampant horses and says, "Lissen, *we* oughta hang out something!" and promptly hangs out an American Eagle, we have no national imagination.)

PB is driving Jean, Ted and me into the country to a stately home on Saturday. He upset me by taking me into a jeweler's to approve a lapel pin he's having made for me. It's gold with the red-and-white crest of the City of London.

Will see him Saturday for the last time, they'll have the pin ready then

*Tuesday, July 20*

I got to Russell Square before Ena, and my friend the ticket taker, after setting up a chair for me, folded his arms behind him, leaned down and inquired conspiratorially:

"Are we anybody we should know?"

Assured him we weren't anybody, and he shook his head reproachfully.

"Painters," he said, "do not paint portraits of Just Anyone."

I told him I was a writer but not famous or important, and he took out a little black book and carefully wrote down my name and Ena's, just as Ena came wobbling round the birdbath with easel, paint box, palette and the mammoth radio she still lugs in case I get bored—though all I ever do with it is make rude remarks about the BBC's taste in music. There's only one classical-music station and whoever runs it is a chamber-music nut, that's all they ever play.

Ena told me I've changed her entire attitude toward portrait painting.

"I never painted anyone out-of-doors before," she said. "The atmosphere and feeling are quite different. From now on I shall have to decide with each subject whether he or she's an outdoors or an indoors subject. You were quite right: you're an outdoors subject."

"We're not out here because I'm an outdoors subject," I said. "We're out here because I'm a selfish subject."

I think she'd love to paint all day long, but no matter what I say, she insists on quitting at one because I have so little time left to see anything.

As we packed up and headed for the station wagon, she looked around Russell Square and said pensively:

"You were right about this place. There's a special quality to it."

It startled me. I'd never said that. Till she said it, I'm not sure I even knew it.

We had lunch at Panzer's and then went back to the National Portrait Gallery, I saw Jane Austen and Leigh Hunt and Willie Hazlitt and the eerie Brontë portrait—the faces of the three sisters and in the middle a gray wash where Bramwell's face once was.

The story is that Bramwell painted himself and his sisters, and then wiped out his own image in a fit of self-hate. And of course you can't concentrate on the sisters' faces, the portrait is dominated by that gray wash in the middle. You can't help wondering whether Bramwell knew it would be.

*Wednesday, July 21*

The Colonel outdid himself again. I'd forgotten that when we passed Stoke Poges on the way to Stratford I'd wanted to detour to see Gray's churchyard just because the "Elegy" was my mother's favorite poem. The Colonel didn't forget; he drove me out to Stoke Poges for dinner, though it's a two-hour drive.

We got there just at twilight. Not a soul around and when we entered the churchyard the bells were tolling the knell of parting day.

Gray's mother is buried there. He wrote the inscription on her monument:

> She had many children of whom only one
> had the misfortune to outlive her.

The church is seven hundred years old, very simple and plain. There were fresh wildflowers in the altar urns. Going down the center aisle you walk on ancient graves of parishioners buried centuries ago beneath the stone floor, their names on the stones obliterated now.

The Colonel strolled the graveyard and let me sit in the church by myself. I wished my mother could know where I was. I felt like the child who calls from a new perch: "Hey, Ma! Look!"

The Colonel's widowed sister-in-law lives near Stoke Poges. She teaches in London and commutes four hours a day, they're as crazy that way here as they are at home. We drove to her house to pick her up for dinner. She lives in a beautiful country suburb that could be anywhere in

Connecticut—as Nora's house and suburb might be anywhere in Queens. It's amazing how alike and anonymous all
suburbs are, as undistinguishable from one another as
highways. Maybe that's why I love cities. There's not a row
of houses in London that could possibly be mistaken for
New York. There isn't a square block of Manhattan that will
ever for a moment remind you of London.

We had dinner at a beautiful pub called The Jolly
Farmer. "Pub" is a very elastic term; it can mean a corner
bar, a bar-and-grill, a cocktail lounge or an expensive
restaurant. The Jolly Farmer is a typical Connecticut
country restaurant: excellent, expensive and relentlessly
charming. I had shrimp curry, and when I told the manager
it was better than the curry I make, he brought me a jar of
his own curry paste to take home to New York.

"Tell me," the Colonel's sister-in-law said to me over
coffee, "why are all Americans so fond of Gray's 'Elegy'?"

Never knew they were, frankly. Except for my mother
I never heard any American mention it. But the Colonel's
sister-in-law meets a much larger cross section of American
tourists at Stoke Poges than I'll ever meet in Manhattan,
and they've all come there because of Gray's "Elegy," so I
took her word for it. And because I didn't have the moral
backbone to say, "I don't know," I explained the whole thing
to her—off the top of my head.

"We are a nation of immigrants," I said. "All our
forebears were the poor and despised masses of Europe and
Africa. We went to school and studied English poetry, and
the poets we read all celebrated the aristocracy: kings and
queens and Sidney's-sister-Pembroke's-mother and the
spires of Oxford and the playing fields of Eton. Except Gray.

Gray celebrated the mute inglorious nobodies. And since all Americans are descended from mute inglorious nobodies, I suppose he strikes a chord with us."

I hope I was right because she and the Colonel believed it. I even believed it myself. Got so carried away by my own eloquence that when we were driving home I began to wonder whether in explaining the American affection for Gray, I'd stumbled on a clue to the English passion for Dickens. They may admire Shakespeare more but it's Dickens they love. Maybe the average Englishman, being neither king nor peasant, identified less with the kings and peasants of Shakespeare than with the lower and middle-class upward-mobility types in Dickens. Even PB shares the national mania for Dickens—but he told me that one of his great-grandfathers was a fishmonger, and that when he was at Eton he was taunted by the other boys because his mother was "a Colonial," born in Australia.

The Colonel is giving a farewell party for me on Sunday night. He'll be at the airport Monday when I leave.

*Thursday, July 22*

I'm getting so guilty about forcing Ena to paint me out-of-doors in London's well-publicized climate. We were rained out this morning for the second time. Yesterday when we were rained out she drove me to the Tower but there were long lines waiting to get in and I still can't stand on line very long. Today we started for the Tower again, but halfway there the weather cleared suddenly and I made her drive back to Russell Square. We'll do the Tower Sunday, I like having it the last London sight I'll see.

My friend the ticket taker is now entirely carried away by the project. He told Ena solemnly:

"That portrait will be worth hoff-a-million one day." I told her if it is I get half.

Leo drove up and found us there at six. I could see Ena grinding her teeth, she'd wanted to paint as long as the light lasted. She'd told him we'd be in Russell Square and he should pick us up for dinner, but she counted on his not finding it till seven; like me, he has no sense of direction. He found Russell Square with no trouble at all and it infuriated her. And dear, obtuse Leo, who worships her and didn't know he'd committed a faux pas, went and committed a worse one: he stood behind her with his hands locked behind his back and gazed profoundly down at the portrait (Ena hates a gallery even if the gallery's Leo) and announced to me that it was "going to be beautiful." That ended the sitting and we drove down to Panzer's, Ena and I in the station wagon, Leo following in the car. He'd wanted to take me somewhere very grand for our farewell dinner but I told him I'd rather have it at Panzer's.

We were finishing our drinks and were trying to find a day for me to drive down to Chartwell, Churchill's old home, which friends of theirs have bought, when I heard someone say:

"Hello, Helene."

I looked up and saw coming toward us a woman I've known casually for years. She runs a successful shop in New York and she's very high-fashion. She's always perfectly friendly and pleasant when we meet but she's never considered me worth more than a passing hello.

I said Well-for-heaven's-sake-Dorothy, and introduced her to Leo and Ena. Leo invited her to join us for dinner, which she did. She explained she's here on a quick buying trip and she'd just landed. Leo, who has the world's most beautiful manners, ordered dinner for her and then engaged her in conversation so Ena and I could work on the Chartwell problem.

The problem was that since I'm leaving on Monday morning I haven't a free day to go down there with them.

"Tomorrow," I told Ena, "Sheila Doel is driving me to Hatfield, it's the only palace I've ever wanted to see; and then we drive back to Highgate for my last dinner with Nora. Saturday is my last day with Pat Buckley, he's taking me somewhere in the country."

"I want the Manns to meet you," said Leo. "If they can have us on Sunday, can you drive down with us then?" And he explained to Dorothy that Christopher Mann and his wife, Eileen Joyce, had bought Chartwell.

"Sunday's the only day we have left for a sitting," I said. "I think Ena's counting on it."

"You need another sitting?" Leo asked, and Ena

nodded, and he explained to Dorothy about the portrait painting.

"I don't see why you have to go home on Monday," said Ena, and sighed. And I sighed. And Leo sighed. And then he turned to Dorothy and asked how long she'd known me. She said vaguely: "I don't know. Eight or ten years."

"Tell me," said Leo in his vibrant English baritone, "we've only known her a few weeks. Why is it so difficult for us to part with her?"

I turned to Dorothy, ready to say something joking, but I never said it. She was literally open-mouthed, gawking at Leo. She mumbled something and then turned her gaze on me, still open-mouthed, still with that incredulous look on her face. Looking at her, I saw my own inward reaction to being a five-week Duchess mirrored in Dorothy's face.

We left Panzer's and Dorothy thanked Leo for dinner and declined a lift to her hotel, she said it was just up the street. Then she turned to me and, struggling to make it sound light and teasing instead of plainly baffled, said:

"I don't suppose there's any use asking you to fit *me* into your busy schedule?"

I wanted to say:

"Never mind, Dorothy. Next week the ball will be over and Cinderella will be back at the pots and pans and typewriter in an old pair of jeans and a hand-me-down T-shirt, same as always."

I just grinned and said I'd see her in New York.

*Friday, July 23*

God bless Sheila, Hatfield House was the crowning touch. It's not the oldest palace or the most beautiful, it's just Elizabeth's. She grew up there. One wing of her palace is still standing, we saw her dining rooms—and more of her kitchens than she ever saw of them.

We sat on a stone bench in the garden. It was quiet and deserted and four hundred years dropped away, you could imagine yourself there in the garden with her when the gentlemen of the Council rode up and dismounted and knelt to tell her she was Queen of England.

We drove back to Highgate for dinner and Nora gave me some photographs of Marks & Co. to take home, and one of Frank. She told me how furious she used to be when he brought one of my letters home to read to the family.

"I'd say to him, 'What kind of husband are you, to bring another woman's letters home!'"

"If he hadn't brought them home," I said, "you'd have had cause to worry."

She looked at me and nodded.

"That's just what Frank used to say," she said.

Her garden almost done; she gave me the last of the roses to bring home.

*Saturday, July 24*

With PB and the Elys to Losely House, an Elizabethan mansion. Elizabeth herself was once a house guest there. And wrote her host a long list of complaints and criticisms when she got home.

The three of them are having dinner tomorrow night at a pub Sam Pepys dined at, they wanted me to come along. I said I'd try to make it before the Colonel's party, I knew perfectly well I couldn't but I'm a coward, I didn't know how to say goodbye-and-thank-you to PB. Will call him tomorrow and say goodbye on the phone.

After we dropped the Elys at the Connaught, he took me to the jeweler's to get my lapel pin. It's a gold crossbar with the red-and-white London seal and the city's motto in gold:

DOMINE DIRIGE NOS

Trust He will go on directing them.

*Sunday, July 25*

Did most of my packing last night so Ena could get an early start in Russell Square this morning, and she painted till noon, when we were rained out again.

She drove me through Regent's Park for a last look at the Nash Crescent and all the lovely streets, and then on down to Panzer's for a farewell lunch before we headed for the Tower.

We drove to the Tower and found people standing on line four abreast, waiting to get in. The line stretched for a city block along the Tower gates, and it wasn't moving. I knew then I would never see the inside of the Tower of London. I could have gone so many times. I let it go too long.

"Next summer," said Ena lightly, "we'll make a list of all the places you didn't see and we'll do the Tower first off!"

She's going to drive me to the airport in the morning.

*Later*

The Colonel has a comfortable flat in Chelsea and his friends are all pleasant and easy to be with: two men, several attractive widows and a shy young couple from Switzerland. I don't remember any of their names or what we talked about, I couldn't concentrate. The party broke up early since I leave for the airport at 10 A.M. Nora was there. She drove me home and we said goodbye and promised to write.

I'm writing this in bed. With the packed suitcase standing open on the floor, the dresser top bare and the drapes drawn against the rain, the room looks exactly as it did the night I came.

Had the suitcase brought down after breakfast and paid the bill. Phoned PB to say goodbye but no answer.

Went up the street to Deutsch's and autographed twenty copies of the book for Australian booksellers due here tomorrow for a convention. Don't know their names and *still* couldn't bring myself just to write my name and let it go at that, it seems unfriendly. Wrote "To an unknown booklover" in every copy, sometimes I think I'm crazy.

Said goodbye to Carmen and Mr. Tammer and all the other people at Deutsch, except André, who hadn't come in yet. Then went over and said goodbye to Russell Square. My friend the ticket taker hadn't come on duty yet; I was there by myself.

Came back to the hotel and tried PB again but still no answer. Decided to write him the minute I get home but would have done that anyway. When I came out of the phone booth Mr. Otto bowed and said solemnly:

"Madam's Jag-U-Ar awaits."

And there was Ena in a borrowed Jag, she said Leo had the car and she wasn't going to drive me to the airport in a station wagon too noisy to talk in.

She gave me a ring set with two small pearls because she once heard me say I like pearls.

The Colonel met us at Heathrow. He had my suitcase taken care of and then led us grandly into the VIP Lounge for sherry. Over sherry, he announced that after my plane left he was going to take Ena on a VIP tour of the airport buildings.

He and Ena walked me to the plane. The Colonel

handed me over to a stewardess and told her to take good care of me, and he and Ena kissed me goodbye. I had a seat by the window and I slid into it and peered out, looking for them. Just as I saw them and lifted my hand to wave, they turned away and vanished in the crowd.

The plane lifted—and suddenly it was as if everything had vanished: Bloomsbury and Regent's Park and Russell Square and Rutland Gate. None of it had happened, none of it was real. Even the people weren't real. It was all imagined, they were all phantoms.

I sit here on the plane trying to see faces, trying to hold onto London, but the mind intrudes with thoughts of home: the mail piled up waiting for me, the people waiting, the world waiting.

Bits of Prospero run in my head:

Our revels now are ended. These our actors
. . . were all spirits and
Are melted into air, into thin air . . .
The cloud-capped towers, the gorgeous palaces,
The solemn temples . . . dissolve
And, like this insubstantial pageant faded,
Leave not a rack behind. We are such stuff
As dreams are made on. . . . .

Rest in peace, Mary Bailey.